Upstart Start-Ups!

ALSO BY RON LIEBER

Taking Time Off: Inspiring Stories of Students
Who Took Successful Breaks from College
and How You Can Plan Your Own
(co-authored with Colin Hall)

UPSTART START-UPS!

How 34 Young Entrepreneurs Overcame Youth, Inexperience, and Lack of Money to Create Thriving Businesses

Ron Lieber

BROADWAY BOOKS New York

Broadway Books titles may be purchased for business or promotional use or for special sales. For information, please write to: Special Markets Department, Bantam Doubleday Dell Publishing Group, Inc., 1540 Broadway, New York, NY 10036.

BROADWAY BOOKS and its logo, a letter B bisected on the diagonal, are trademarks of Broadway Books, a division of Bantam Doubleday Dell Publishing Group, Inc.

Library of Congress Cataloging-in-Publication Data

Lieber, Ron
Upstart start-ups! : how 34 young entrepreneurs overcame youth, inexperience, and lack of money to create thriving businesses / by Ron Lieber. — 1st ed.
p. cm.
Includes index.
ISBN 0-7679-0088-X (pbk.)
1. New business enterprises. 2. New business enterprises—Case studies. 3. Entrepreneurship. I. Title.
HD62.5.L53 1998
658′.041—dc21 98-17647
CIP

FIRST EDITION

Designed by Susan Hood

98 99 00 01 02 10 9 8 7 6 5 4 3 2 1

CONTENTS

CHAPTER 1

WHAT IT TAKES (AND WHAT IT DOESN'T)

The Traits Upstarts Share

What do you want to be when you grow up? At first glance, this might seem like a strange question to be asking in a book like this. Books about starting your own business usually begin with the assumption that you're a risk taker who desperately wants to get rich quick. (After all, what other reason would there be to work for yourself?) So the books unfold, leaving you with a few hundred pages by hucksterish millionaires telling you how to sell like a pro.

This isn't that sort of book, because entrepreneurship isn't just about get-rich-quick schemes anymore. As the job market has changed over the last decade, most of us who are under 35 or so have begun to approach our careers with a new set of criteria.

Once upon a time, you could count on job security in return for a job well done. Today, many of us have come to accept the fact that we could be fired at any time. In other words, placing your bets on a career with a big company carries just as much risk as starting your own. Turning to entrepreneurship has become a career choice like any other. It's fraught with the usual confusion and despair that any job you have early in your career will hold, but it also puts your fate in your own hands.

So this isn't a book about people who have gotten rich quick. Instead, it's about ordinary people, young Americans who started businesses without the benefit of a trust fund or a Bill Gates–sized brain, written for people who are trying to do it themselves.

DO WHAT YOU LOVE

So do you want to be an entrepreneur when you grow up? One of the oft-repeated maxims of the adult world says that entrepreneurs are born, not made. Bullshit. Just because you didn't grow up peddling newspapers or making barrettes to sell to your friends doesn't mean that you lack the necessary entrepreneurial instinct.

As you may know already from having jumped around in the job market some, one of the best ways to make career decisions is through the process of elimination. If you can figure out a few things that you absolutely do not want to do, you have already discovered something truly helpful. "I've met with and talked to other people who have started a business in an area that they don't truly love," notes Tom Gardner, who at age 26 launched the Motley Fool, an online personal finance forum, with his brother David. "Most of them are desperately trying to get out by selling their businesses for cash in order to start something that they really care about. You want to begin in business by trying to get as close as possible to the things with which you're truly obsessed." After all, if the underlying product or service you're offering doesn't totally turn you on, it's going to be hard to motivate yourself to do all the grunt work to support it. If you can't imagine your fledgling business thrilling you five or ten years from now, you're better off working nine to five for someone else.

You don't have to find the right thing to do the first time around, but you should at least be close. Take Tom Scott, one of the founders of juice maker Nantucket Nectars. Well before he and his partner whipped up their first batch of peach nectar, he had begun to understand that he might be better off working for himself. "If I was working for someone else, I always fell in the middle to low range of employee competence," he recalls. "We loved the water, so we started a business delivering groceries and supplies to boats in Nantucket Harbor." That was the summer of 1988, when Scott was just 22 years old. It wasn't until his partner, Tom First, suggested that they start selling their drinkable fruit concoction that the partners transformed themselves from delivery boys into something completely different. Both pursuits involved something that they loved; one just turned out to be about a thousand times more lucrative.

KISSING OFF CORPORATE BOSSES

The two Toms were fortunate in that they both knew early on that they wanted to work for themselves one day. You may not be so sure right off the bat, however, or it may take some bad experiences working for a company that someone else started to convince you that you'd be better off launching your own. Today, Ava

DeMarco owns Little Earth, a Pittsburgh-based manufacturer of handbags and other accessories made from recycled goods, with her husband, Rob Brandagee. But she began her career as a graphic designer at a firm with two partners, where she soon became the third owner. "One would approach me about getting rid of the other partner, and then that other one would come in scheming about doing the same thing. Their business ethics just didn't jibe with mine," she recalls. "I suggested time sheets to see who was actually doing all the work, since we were splitting up the profits equally. But they said that keeping track of hours would ruin things because it would mean that we didn't trust one another. I just kept thinking that things were already ruined and if it were my firm, I'd be doing things very differently."

Before Amy Nye Wolf started Altitunes, a chain of airport-based music stores, she too fell in with someone who taught her a lot about how not to run a small business. After working for Goldman Sachs, a big investment firm in New York City, she had lots of job offers but chose to go with a small market research firm that studied the spending habits of young people. "My boss was a total nut," she says now. "I thought that by going to work for a small company it would be my chance to make an impact. But she would fudge our survey results and exaggerate the number of people we had interviewed when making presentations to clients. Then when I left after fulfilling my year-long commitment to her, she tried to pay me less than she had promised me."

Personality problems are often only the beginning. One of the biggest problems with spending your first years in the working world toiling away for others is that no matter how smart you are, you'll probably be doing a lot of shit work. Before she started an art gallery called Clementine, Abby Messitte worked as an assistant in a fancy gallery in New York City's Soho neighborhood. "Despite my art degrees from Amherst and Columbia, there I was answering phones, taking dictation, and picking up dry cleaning," she says. "It was demeaning, but I was also terrified, since it turned out that I was really bad at all these mundane tasks." The gallery's owners finally just up and fired her after a few months, claiming that she "didn't take enough initiative." Was she supposed to be doing more mundane tasks of her own volition? "Cooking up this gallery scheme was my way of proving that they were wrong," she says. Not to mention spending her days doing something infinitely more challenging.

"The real problem," adds Elizabeth Burke, Messitte's partner in Clementine, "is the job outlook for anyone in their 20s. There's so little out there in between the low-level assistant jobs and the high-level stuff."

As you probably know by now, even having a decent job doesn't guarantee that you'll end up feeling satisfied with it. David Gardner (of Motley Fool fame) had a job writing for a financial newsletter published by Louis Rukeyser, who hosts an influential, nationally televised show about the stock market. "I wrote about the things that I have a lot of passion about," he says, noting how much better you write when you have a burning interest in the topic at hand.

Even so, he still ran into lots of politics. "Take a story I wrote about discount brokers. Don't you think if you're making your own decisions about which stocks to buy that you shouldn't have to pay full commission on your stock trades to a fancy stockbroker? Well, I got the article I had written about this subject back, and what I had written was condensed into the first half of the story. Then in the second half, the editor had added all these reasons why using discount brokers might be a bad idea." The same thing happened when Gardner touted Quicken, the personal finance software that later swept America. "After ten months, I was out of there." As Gardner knows, people don't want nuanced personal finance writing. They want to know where to put their money once they're finished reading. Today, millions of people turn to Motley Fool for just that sort of advice, scanning its forums on different stocks and industries and reading its irreverent commentary.

This sort of tension has always existed when young, smart employees run up against an entrenched system. They tend to get pushed into entrepreneurship when that frustration is combined with the desire to avoid the pain and disillusionment their parents experienced during their own years in the working world. "We've seen the people on television and in the newspapers who were laid off when they were 50 years old," notes Andy Spade, who with his wife, Kate, started Kate Spade, a handbag company, in 1993 when they were both in their late 20s. "We both knew what it was like to struggle, to have to work our way through school. Kate had just seven dollars when she first got to New York City. We didn't want to go through all that anymore. We wanted to chase our own destiny."

To have some sort of control over one's own fate is often what young entrepreneurs want. "What became so appealing to me about running my own business was that I was in control," says Robert Stephens, who started a Minneapolis computer repair firm called Geek Squad when he was 24. "So if I made an improvement in the system, I received all the benefits." Of course he would also receive the summons from bankruptcy court if the business tanked, but at least his fate would be more or less in his own hands.

"My dad really didn't like his job at General Motors," adds Kevin Donlin, who started a company called Guaranteed Resumes when he was 30 years old. "But he did it for 37 years because he saw himself as a provider. He did provide well for us, but he'd come home exhausted and bitching about it all the time. I couldn't stand the thought of getting stuck doing something I hated for someone else for that long."

ARE YOU EXPERIENCED?

So you're convinced that you want to bet your career on an up-start start-up? Before you fling your doors open, it's important to ask yourself whether you've really got what it takes to pull it off. Many older people will try to tell you that you need a lot of work experience before you can launch a successful business. And it's true that it does help. Working in the real estate department at Goldman Sachs before she started Altitunes gave Amy Nye Wolf some killer negotiating skills to draw on once she began hammering out airport leases for her music kiosks. But don't be intimidated or swayed by those well-meaning people who would urge you to get the same seasoning. Microsoft, Kinko's Copies, and Yahoo are just a few of the businesses started by people with no business experience at all. You could do worse.

Similarly, you might think that if you don't take business classes somewhere along the way you'll be at a disadvantage. Maybe you should get an M.B.A. first, right? Well, even if you do, it may not be as helpful as you think. "Every single thing about the way we started our company was totally opposite of the way they taught us to do it in business school," says Gary Alpert, cofounder of Wet Feet Press, a San Francisco company that publishes insider guides to various corporations for people preparing for job interviews there. Although Alpert and his partner, Steve Pollock, have M.B.A.'s from Stanford, perhaps the best business school on earth, they still didn't do things by the book. "They tell you that you have to have venture capital lined up, that you have to have a business plan, that you have to have a board of advisors. We didn't have time for any of that. We came up with the idea in October, and we needed to have products by January."

In fact, your choice of curriculum in school may ultimately mean very little. Julia Stern, co-owner of Malia Mills, a swimwear designer in New York City, discovered this as an undergraduate at Cornell. "I started in arts and sciences, but I was impatient with its lack of relevance to real life, so I ended up transferring to the hotel and restaurant school there," she explains. "While I had an up-and-down relationship with that part of the university as well, the most fascinating thing about it was the constant stream of alumni coming through to give lectures on the hotels and restaurants they had started. Real people working in real life—that's what I found interesting."

Stern ended up at *Sports Illustrated* working on the annual swimsuit issue, after which she soon grew restless and eventually found her calling. Tom Baron, however, was an upstart from the get go. After a brief period as a used car salesmen, he started a home delivery service for several Pittsburgh restaurants. Eventually, he and a friend opened their own dining spot, a rollicking joint called Mad Mex. "If you want to be in high finance, maybe you need your M.B.A.," Baron says. "But if you're going to start out as street fighters like we are, it's not going to do anything for you. I'm not patient enough to see things in that logical progression: go to business school, work for a while, get experience. I've got to have it. I've just got to do it."

Indeed, one of the biggest complaints about traditional business schools is that they place so much emphasis on risk avoidance. That can dampen the enthusiasm of fledgling entrepreneurs in class. "School in general has an effect which counteracts your ability to think on your own," explains Tom Scott of Nantucket Nectars. "School gives you the rules of the game, and you begin to believe that they can't be changed, because if there were any better ones out there, well then of course they would be teaching them."

Others are more harsh in their criticism. Take Geek Squad's Robert Stephens, who worked in a computer lab as an undergraduate at the University of Minnesota before launching his company. "I worked with a bunch of Ph.D.'s," he says, "and they were the laziest motherfuckers I had ever seen. They'd show up at eleven in the morning, take a two-hour lunch, and didn't do anything afterwards. Meanwhile, I'd work 48 hours straight, because I saw my meal ticket. Even if I didn't ever graduate [which he didn't], I knew that if I worked hard enough at the lab I'd pick up so many skills that I'd be able to get a job anywhere."

Of course, most people who achieve fabulous success without having shelled out the big bucks for tuition believe strongly in the rightness of their ways. But those who have the degrees almost always give at least some credit to the things they learned in the classroom. Alpert, for all his hustle to enter his market without regard for the Stanford rules of start-ups, notes that his M.B.A. *has* helped him with many other aspects of running the business. And John Chuang, cofounder of MacTemps, which specializes in temps trained to work on Macintosh computers, has an M.B.A. as well, and the way he approached business school may be a good model to emulate.

MacTemps evolved from a business Chuang ran with some friends as an undergraduate at Harvard in the mid-1980s. The business school was impressed enough with his accomplishments to offer him admission right after he finished his bachelor's degree, a very rare occurrence. Chuang was so gung ho about his company that he put Harvard off for three years until it threatened to withdraw its offer of admission. Sure, he could have blown it off at that point, since his business was already successful. But he had a hunch that continuing his education might help bring it to a whole new level. "You have to remember, I had never worked anywhere else other than at my own company," he says now. "So I knew how small entrepreneurial companies worked. That wasn't the problem. Knowing those things at that point wasn't as useful to me as knowing how big companies like General Electric ran and how they had grown from a small entrepreneurial company to a big company."

The only question was whether Chuang would be able to do both things at once. "I had been promising myself that I wouldn't go to school and run the business at the same time," he says. The compromise: attend class full-time and spend ten hours a week at the MacTemps office, which was right down the street. "Not only did I end up getting a lot out of the program, but the whole staff did too," he explains. "I'd be working on a case study in class and would get really psyched up and come back to the office and tell everyone about it. Then we'd sit around and talk about how the issues might apply here." Plus, Chuang made MacTemps the subject of all his homework. As a result, he got a lot of free advice from his professors and classmates when it came time to discuss specific issues his business was facing.

THE IMPORTANCE OF BEING CLUELESS

Business school or no, the decision to start a company should involve some pretty serious soul-searching. After all, it's not just your training that bears on whether your venture will be successful. Your mind-set is pretty important too. So whom do you need to be? What sort of personality traits should you have?

When Tom Scott of Nantucket Nectars asks himself these questions, he thinks about a family friend he visited early in his company's life. "This was someone who came back from the war and started in a gas station and ended up running Getty Petroleum," he says. "His whole career was made by sticking his neck out, having no clue how to do whatever it was he had to do next, and then going ahead and doing it anyway." Scott believes that the ability to achieve in the face of overwhelming cluelessness begins with a burning curiosity. "The thing that stuck with me from the first day we started was the rush, the fact that things were changing all the time, that every day was something new. We figured out the glass bottles and the caps and the labels and came up with a way to communicate with our customers. And the more we picked up steam, the more that rush increased because we realized that we really could figure out how to solve whatever problems came up."

It helps to be able to visualize the end product, whether it's a great-looking, great-tasting bottle of juice or a nice piece of consulting work. "When I'm at point A, I can see point E, and I don't get stuck on what will happen at B, C, and D," says Scott. "Ninety percent of the people in the general population are so focused on what might go wrong in the middle that they lose sight of their goals." Or, as Andrew Koven, who started Collegiate Sales and Marketing, a company that created marketing campaigns aimed at college students, puts it: "You want to be like a bull in a china shop, because the one piece left standing after you've stormed through is usually worth more than anything else."

It's crucial that the right sorts of goals and values are driving that vision. Money can be a great motivator, to be sure. Dave Kapell started making magnetic poetry kits for the refrigerators of his friends and acquaintances in Minneapolis because he was close to defaulting on his student loans. And Robert Stephens, who worked in a custom-made bedding store before starting Geek Squad, is motivated to this day in part by a self-made millionaire who came into the shop once. "This guy was 32 years old and had just decided to retire for a decade or two to enjoy his money while he was young," he recalls. "We were doing a circular mattress for his yacht. I don't know where he is now, but I'm going to thank him one day. Every time I'm up late working and get paged two dozen times by my customers, I think about him, and every time I do I'm getting that much closer to catching up to him in the Caribbean."

A little red-blooded capitalism never hurt anyone, and it's clear from talking to Stephens and seeing his relatively modest lifestyle that his goals are not about greed. Instead, he's just homing in on that point E that Tom Scott strives to reach. As far as Scott is concerned, that end point should have little to do with money. "To me this is just an alternative way of making a paycheck so I don't have to work for somebody else," he says. "I wonder if people who are so focused on what their company would be worth if they sold it right then and there can really be successful in the long run." At the very least, it's smart to expect very delayed financial gratification.

As Scott's partner, Tom First, points out, it's really sort of a useless exercise anyway. "Look," he says, "the only value of your company is what somebody might pay you for it one day, but if you're not interested in selling it then the question is moot. The magic of these last few years was that there was no value to our time, no value placed on our energy. The only thing we focused on was how much further we could push the company."

I BELIEVE THAT CHILDREN ARE OUR FUTURE

You may have noticed that one thing many of these young entrepreneurs have in common is a healthy dose of self-confidence. While it's true that a measured bit of egotism helps when you're trying to do something better or quicker or more uniquely than it's ever had done before, what's central here is the overarching attitude that confidence gives birth to. "One thing that distinguishes potential entrepreneurs is an effusive sort of optimism," says Motley Fool's David Gardner. "There are people in the world who can't see how anything will ever work out, or just think it will be too much of a pain in the ass to do it. And then there are the people who think all of life is wonderful and work so hard because of those feelings that they have. Ultimately, it's not a value judgment. I mean, maybe optimism is just a flight of fancy and we'd all be better off if we were pessimists. But when you're talking about starting your own business, you have to be one of those people who believes you can do anything if you set your mind to it."

"There was never a point where I didn't think I could make it work," notes Todd Alexander, owner of a wine distributorship in

Atlanta called Vendemmia. "Ignorance is bliss. As long as I had a place to store the wine and a truck to deliver it in, I believed that eventually I would sell it at a profit. This isn't rocket science. My business doesn't hinge on some technical development that may or may not occur. People have been growing grapes and making wine for many years. I just happen to sell it."

Alexander's confidence aside, it's hard to ignore the naysayers who insist that most small businesses fail within a couple years. Indeed, failure is everywhere in the business world, so you might as well face up to the fact that you'll make some significant screwups. "Failure is a natural by-product of success," insists Andrew Koven, whose marketing company had a few hiccups along the way. "You have to be prepared to take some blows," adds Elizabeth Burke, whose art gallery is still standing even though she and her partner have had artists snatched out from under them and have pissed off a collector or two.

Lately, some venture capitalists have surmised that failure is an essential forerunner to success, so they examine the backgrounds of the entrepreneurs who want their money in the hopes of finding a character-building, lesson-bedecked disaster in their past. That's not to say that you should tank your first entrepreneurial outing just to build your résumé. But ask yourself some tough questions. "Start by assuming you won't make it," suggests Jeffrey Hyman, cofounder of Career Central for MBAs, a company that matches M.B.A.s with job openings. "Then ask yourself if everything you think you'll learn along the way is worth it. I feel like with all that we've been through here, it would make me that much more marketable. If this thing tanks, I'll have another job the next day." As Hyman suggests, that which does not kill your business will only make you stronger. And even if it does slay the thing, you won't be labeled a failure. You'll simply be considered more "experienced."

Sorry, there's that word again. Sure, hundreds of years of history document the success of pushcart capitalism, with young salesmen and tradespeople scraping out a living by hustling in the streets. Still, ever since the dawn of the modern American corporation several decades back, young people have been warned to get some experience—lots of it—before attempting to start their own companies. Only recently, as more and more people under 35 have ignored these admonitions and achieved amazing success as a result, has it become clear just how foolish it can be.

"Just take a look at baseball," says Motley Fool's David Gardner. "What's the peak age? You'd probably be tempted to say that it's 31 or 32. But really it's 27. Still, when somebody young messes up there it's a 'rookie mistake.' But when a veteran makes the same error, it's just 'Aw, tough break.' That is such crap!

"I'm a 'celebrate-youth' guy. I've never placed any stock in age. I really believe that as individuals, our business peak is at about age 27. It's not 48, and it's definitely not 62, which is the age of a lot of CEOs. Our business is particularly good for proving that point because our model stock portfolio is out there for everyone to inspect and it's doing well. But there are standards in every business, and that's all that should matter in a true, pure meritocracy. If you perform, you win. That's how it should be. Not how old are you. Not how good-looking you are. But how good you are. That's the way life should be."

How is it possible that you, with little or no business experience, could be at your peak right now? "When we were first out on our little skiff, servicing boats in Nantucket Harbor, we had an innocence and a drive that I have never had before and I have never had since," says Nantucket Nectars's Tom Scott. "We just started our first retail business, a juice bar, and the guy who's running it for us just took us on a tour of the store. I could see it in his eyes—the excitement, the pride. I mean, I get excited too, but it's pretty brief now. People do lose it, but right now, he'll go through walls to make that place work. That's good for us now, and it was good for us back when it was just the two of us trying to make the business work." Adds his partner, Tom First: "If Nantucket Nectars disappeared tomorrow and we tried to set up something similar to replace it, I'm not sure we could do it. We know too much now, and we'd probably be too careful."

The bliss of ignorance is just the beginning, however. While lots of adults treated First and Scott like cute kids attempting to start a scaled-up lemonade stand, one person in particular took them very seriously. He reminded them of something well worth remembering. "Early on, one of the guys who had founded Stride Rite shoes happened to be at my parents' house one night for a dinner party, so I showed him what we were doing," recalls First. "He looked at me and said, 'God, this is so great. You have got to keep at this, because you will never be able to do something like this again.' "

Think about it. You want to start a company at some point in your life—a big financial risk and a huge commitment of time no matter how you look at it. Isn't it better to do it now, when you're less likely to have a spouse and children and own big things like a house that can be taken away from you if your business blows up? It's a no-brainer. "Whenever someone remarks on how amazing it is that we pulled this off when we were so young," says Scott, "I always respond that it's much more amazing when someone does it while they're in their 40s."

Not only does age tend to add responsibility to people's lives, it can also cause them to get set in their ways. There's a famous story about Henry Ford trying to figure out how to speed up his assembly line. When told by his team of grizzled engineers that they couldn't make things go any faster, he reportedly shouted, "Well gosh darn it, then go get me some 25-year-olds who don't know that it can't be done!" Explains Marcia Kilgore, who owns a spa in New York City called Bliss: "The great advantage of being young is that you're not jaded. I'm always hearing from fashion editors and other people about how I'm so positive, that I think anything can happen. Well yeah, exactly. Why not? Be smart, find your niche, make it happen. I never think about why something hasn't been done already; I think about why nobody has done it right yet."

What Kilgore is referring to is simple agility, for the younger you are, the fewer rules you have to unlearn. The success of the Gardner brothers and their Motley Fool site on America Online (which is now on the World Wide Web, too) is the perfect example. "If there's some larger change in the business environment, like what has been happening in the online world, the biggest businesses are always going to be the slowest to adjust," says Tom Gardner. "They're not going to take the risk of having a big point-and-click button on the computer screen that says 'Fool' instead of 'ABC.' These companies take young people, put them on the online staff, and say, 'Whatever you do, don't screw up! Don't take any risks!' And there we were in the middle of it all with our hearts on our sleeves."

With youth comes some other helpful attributes too. If you know anyone who's ever started a business, you understand how important sheer stamina is. "Youth hasn't held us back, because our energy level is so high," says Pam Schmick, who owns a rock-climbing gym in Bloomington, Illinois, with her husband, Chris. "Our employees and customers feed off it because they've seen what we can do."

Perhaps the biggest thing you have on your side as a relative youngster is patience. Sure, there might be some student loan payments left, but at least you're not facing down college bills for your own children. Retirement is a long way off. You've got half a century to make this business of yours work. And it's a good thing. "You barely even see the rewards right away," notes Andy Spade. "You can go from one million to five million in sales in one year, and then hit ten the year after that. But it may take many years to get to one million in the first place, and if you give up before that happens, you obviously won't ever get there."

Older folks may not have the time to wait that long, which is why it's a damn good thing that you're not one of them.

CHAPTER 2

THE LIGHTBULB CHAPTER

Where Do Great Ideas Come from Anyway?

Nothing is done.... Everything in the world remains to be done or done over.... The greatest picture is not yet painted, the greatest play isn't written, the greatest poem is unsung. There isn't in all the world a perfect railroad, nor a good government, nor a sound law. Physics, mathematics, and especially the most advanced and exact of sciences, are being fundamentally revised. Chemistry is just becoming a science; psychology, economics, and sociology are awaiting a Darwin, whose work in turn is awaiting an Einstein.... If the rah-rah boys in our colleges could be told this, they might not all be specialists in football, parties, and unearned degrees. They are not told it, however; they are told to learn what is known. This is nothing.

—*Lincoln Steffens*

I know, I know. The other thing we're all told in college is to kill as much space as possible by starting an essay with some pompous, long-winded quote. But seriously, this Steffens guy makes a lot of sense. A turn-of-the-century muckracker turned communist sympathizer, he may not have meant to be an entrepreneurial guru. Still, it's hard not to feel psyched up about your place in the world if you really think about what he's saying here. There's a lot of new stuff left to make and do in the world, and even more that can be fixed and made better. No matter where you look, there are bound to be lots of great business ideas.

So how do you open your eyes to the opportunities? This is another area where young people have distinct advantages. Not so long ago, you were a little kid with lots of questions. Or you may have one or two small children yourself now, so you're reliving it once more. While kids can certainly get preoccupied pondering imponderables, like the color of the sky or the philosophy of early bedtimes, they ask a lot of good questions. Often, great businesses begin simply with a childlike question about why something is the way it is and why it can't be any different or better. Your memories of what it was like to be that age and think that way are twice as fresh as those of baby boomers twice your age. So pretend you're a kid, and ask away.

DO WHAT YOU KNOW (AND KNOW WHAT YOU DO)

To start with, ask yourself what expertise you already have that could become the launching point for a business. "Do what you know" has always been some of the best career advice out there, and it applies particularly well to entrepreneurial endeavors. People who love to cook have a much better chance of starting a successful catering business than they do going into heavy industry. They're also liable to find it a lot more interesting. "Sure, it may be true that all the mom-and-pop metal scrapyards in the world should be consolidated into a single billion-dollar business," says Altitunes's Amy Nye Wolf, "but that doesn't mean you in particular are going to want to wake up and do that every day."

Kate Spade had been an accessories editor for Mademoiselle magazine for several years, selecting handbags and other things to use in the background of magazine photos, when inspiration struck her and her boyfriend, Andy, in 1992. "There was a lot of retro-looking, cutesy-ish lady stuff out there at the time," she recalls. "Many fashion people make these teeny-tiny bags for this small group of customers. It's all just about saying to everyone else in the design community, 'Hey, look what I can do.'

"But what I kept seeing in my head was larger—a square or a rectangle—and it was strong-looking, almost like a suitcase. It wasn't precious, it didn't have a lot of hardware, maybe it was nylon or straw, but higher quality than something you'd buy on the beach in Mexico. Somewhere between L.L. Bean and Prada—preppy, but more artful than the Ralph Lauren blue blazer kind of look. More John Kennedy than Prince Charles. It was a bag I wanted to own, and I couldn't find it anywhere."

Marcia Kilgore started her career as a personal trainer in Manhattan. Having grown up in Saskatchewan, there wasn't a whole lot to do other than play hockey or work out. After three years of passing on her weightlifting knowledge, she turned to another area where she had even more personal experience. "I had bad skin for a long time, and I never really knew how to take care of it," she recalls. "Everything I tried didn't work, and every morning I'd wake up and want to cry when I looked in the mirror. So I decided I'd take a skin care course, just for myself. I figured it might be fun to give skin treatments to my friends too, but once they found out I knew how to do them, they wanted facials and their friends were calling me too. So I started to charge people." Since then, her spa, Bliss, has outgrown a couple different locations in New York and now attracts hundreds of women each week, and some men too.

While David and Tom Gardner had done a bit of investing in the stock market in high school and college, that alone was not enough to give them the skills to dole out investment advice to hundreds of thousands of people on the Motley Fool. "The foundation of what we're doing here today is a dice baseball game called Strat-O-Matic," says Tom. "We had a league while we were growing up outside Washington, D.C. Everyone would have their own team that they had drafted from the pool of real baseball players that year. All 26 people would come over to our house on the weekend. And pretty much all day Saturday and Sunday we would spread out over our bedroom floors and play.

"It was a numbers game, and we kept lots of stats. There were so many different variables, just like the stock market has and just like businesses have. And it was also a people thing, which is a big part of running a business, because all the fun of it was making trades with your competitors, some of whom knew nothing about baseball and some of whom were masters of it.

"That's the same spirit that's here at the company now. I mean, obviously, it's a lot more serious, but sometimes when I look out on the office floor, it's almost like we've got a big game going here and everyone has their responsibilities. It's that same gaming spirit that we knew growing up, both in terms of how we view the market and how we run the business."

The idea for the original Motley Fool newsletter was not born over a boyhood game of baseball per se. That came later, as David grew frustrated with his job writing for the Rukeyser newsletter. But the model for the business, as you can see, was derived from a sort of gamesmanship that the brothers had known and mastered long ago.

DO WHAT NEEDS TO BE DONE

For anyone working with computers, whether it's hardware or software or technical skills, the last decade has obviously been a great time to be starting companies. Because the desktop computer revolution took place when most of us were teenagers, we had a chance to gain as much experience working on the machines as anyone two or three times our age. While John Chuang was an undergraduate at Harvard in the Macintosh-crazed mid-1980s, he and some friends did desktop publishing work and used the proceeds to buy a laser printer (a $5,000 purchase at the time) and some top-of-the-line Macs on which to do the work for their clients. Rather than let the computers sit around all day while they were in class, they opened a small storefront and put their friends to work renting out the Macs on a per-hour basis. They also charged people to run things off on the laser printer, since fancy printers like that were not widely available at the time.

It was a nice little business, but when Chuang and his partners graduated, they realized that they couldn't all make a living off it at the same time. "We were scared to death," he recalls. "This was 1987, right before the stock market crash, and all our friends were working on Wall Street making $50,000 a year doing mergers and acquisitions and getting wined and dined. And there we were in this ratty building with ratty carpeting. We were paying ourselves $300 per week, but that's really all the money there was, so we knew the business had to grow up fast."

About that time, a curious thing began to happen. "We still had the desktop publishing business, and occasionally clients would call us up and ask us to come out to their site and help them out," says Chuang. "They knew we knew how to use the Macs pretty well, so whenever they had problems installing software or keeping their systems from crashing, they would call us up."

Almost by accident, a temporary agency was born. "I had worked as a temp before college, so I knew how the basics of the business worked—what to charge, what to pay people, that sort of thing," Chuang recalls. "So when these calls started coming, we figured, all right, if there's a demand for our services, why not hire ourselves out? I had always sort of admired the business model, because the agencies get a cut of each temp's check. It seemed to require very little work on the agency's part, which greatly appealed to me."

Little did he know what was about to happen. The Macintosh community in Boston was fairly tight-knit at the time and it seemed small to Chuang when he attended various Mac user meetings. Nonetheless, he figured it couldn't hurt to spend $70 to take out a quarter-page ad in the local Mac newsletter. Chuang and his partners settled on a name, MacTemps, and ran an ad that said "You didn't buy just any computer. Why hire just any temp to use it?"

The impact was immediate. "The phones started ringing, and they just never stopped," says Chuang. "We should have been surprised, but we were just too excited. But then we realized we had no one to send out, so we sent ourselves out, which is exactly what we were trying to avoid in the first place. We sent all our friends too. We even sent customers from our store who seemed smart and wanted to make some extra money. Anyone we could find." Though Chuang didn't have quite enough bodies at the time, he knew instantly that if this idea was working in Boston, it might also work in every large city in the world.

Andrew Koven, the college marketer, had a similar problem when he first got started. While he had an intuitive sense of how to sell, at first, like Chuang, he hadn't hit on the correct thing to be selling. As an undergraduate at Syracuse and for a few years afterwards, Koven had built up a nice business moving the belongings of college students in and out of storage each term. But what he also had were some great marketing campaigns in place to reach them, complete with campus sales reps, event sponsorships, and lots of advertising. In other words, Koven had a tremendous working knowledge of how to reach a lucrative niche market: college students. He just didn't know that that was his greatest strength.

So how did he discover that there was a collegiate marketing firm lurking within the confines of his storage business? Companies that needed to reach the same students he was already communicating with contacted him and told him so. "They saw that I understood how to get college students to go out and sell things," he says. "I had set up an infrastructure that could support that. The medium I was in was storage, but the raw materials there—the students—were reconfigurable. We could set them up to sell ski packages, promote a book, anything." His first client was Jones Soda, a gourmet beverage company that was looking for young salespeople to act as reps to stores and shopkeepers near college campuses.

Alex Kramer is another example of someone who didn't realize she had a great business idea until people started begging her to help them out. After graduating from George Washington University, she took a job as a paralegal for a Washington, D.C., law firm. After less than a year, her mother ran into a friend who was working as a private investigator and needed someone to replace her when she moved away. One thing led to another, and soon Kramer was working for the investigating firm.

Over the next few years, Kramer worked for three different firms—doing research on the opposition for political campaigns, working for unions investigating management during labor negotiations, and digging around in courthouse basements. She also learned how to do surveillance work, which she insists is a lot less exciting than it sounds. Eventually, she developed a reputation as an expert in public records searches, hunting down everything from legal documents to unlisted phone numbers.

Kramer's third job ended when the two partners in the firm she was working for split up. While she had kept her network from her previous jobs alive, no one had a full-time job to offer her. Still, they had a lot of projects available on a freelance basis, and Kramer began to pick some of them up. "I had no expenses, so I was able to float for a while with the project work," she recalls. "Somehow this thing started to evolve, and I got busier and busier. People at my earlier jobs were giving out my name to colleagues who needed help, and I just kept at it. I never declared myself in business for myself. I didn't have any goals to start my own business. It just had never crossed my mind. I just called myself a freelancer. But after a certain point, you're a business owner and not just a freelancer. I'm not sure what the difference is, but eventually I got some letterhead and stationery and began to market myself."

The incidence of this sort of accidental entrepreneurship is less rare than you might think. Often, people have no idea that the skill they use so well as a full-time employee for someone else could simply be auctioned off to the highest bidder every couple weeks. And then, suddenly, you're a consultant or a free agent or a one-person temporary agency.

Lots of people do this on purpose too. Before Kevin Donlin decided to start his own business at age 30, he had worked as a manager in a record store, played in a band, acquired a teaching certificate, taught English in Japan, and worked as a writer for a marketing firm in Minneapolis. So what did this all add up to? "At first I thought I wanted to start an import/export business to draw on my experience overseas," he says. "But I kept coming back to the fact that there would be all these costs associated with keeping whatever products I had around, so I would have to price whatever I was selling accordingly to recover those inventory costs.

"Eventually, I came to the idea of helping people with their résumés. I had always been pretty good at the employment game and never had much trouble finding a new job when I needed one. When I looked at samples of some of the work that other people were doing in that area, I wasn't all that impressed. I knew I could out-write these people, and the business seemed like it would be a great mix of using both those writing skills and my teaching skills. It also solved the inventory problem that I would have had with import/export, since the only inventory was me."

Donlin also knew from experience how desperately needed his skills were. "My first résumé out of college was just dreadful," he recalls. "It was what I refer to now as a tombstone résumé—just names, dates, and places with nothing to tell anyone about the person behind it. Ten years later, that's still what I see from most of my clients, even the ones who have been out of college and in the working world for a long time. You never get enough sense of their accomplishments, their skills, and their personality."

This is an interesting twist on the "do what you know" model. Call it the "teach what you know now but didn't know then that could have been really useful at the time" school of starting and running a business. When Gary Alpert and Steve Pollock graduated from Stanford Business School, they used this model to tap a market need that no one had ever thought to exploit. Though neither of them took a permanent job after graduating from business school, they were amazed that their friends who were going off to

Microsoft and Morgan Stanley had found no central resource for useful information on those companies during their job searches. Sure, all those corporations have glossy recruiting brochures. But no one had ever bothered to produce an insider guide to getting hired and working at one of these places, designed especially for people in their 20s and 30s. From that realization, Wet Feet Press was born.

Jeffrey Hyman, founder of Career Central for MBAs, discovered another niche to fill in the same industry based on his own job-hunting frustrations. As he was getting ready to graduate from business school at Northwestern University in Chicago, Hyman knew he wanted to land a job doing marketing for a high-tech company. However, few of the good ones recruited in the Midwest, and headhunters weren't interested in helping someone with little experience. Though Hyman ended up with a great job at Intuit, the maker of Quicken and other personal finance software, it was only the result of his own pluck—calling hundreds of people and flying around to interview at his own expense.

"It was in the course of that job search that I first realized that there was an opportunity there," Hyman recalls. "All these great high-tech companies and other smaller companies were out there, I was someplace else, and no one was putting us together efficiently. Not everyone has the time and money and wherewithal to fly around and find them the way I had done. As far as headhunters go, I had helped hire people for the company I worked with before business school. So I knew that while they charge at least one-quarter of your hire's first-year salary, most of them take a long time to come up with names of candidates and don't add much value short of shuffling a lot of résumés around."

Lun Yuen, whom Hyman eventually brought in as a partner,

had seen similar problems as a long-time Intuit employee. "We'd look at a stack of 200 résumés, and maybe two would be interesting," he says. "In the meantime, all these headhunters would call me and totally waste my time and theirs because they never had any idea what kind of job I might be interested in leaving Intuit for. So one of the things I had taken away from just dealing with these issues over the years is that trying to find good people tends to be a totally random, inefficient process."

So what would happen if someone came up with a way to start with a pool of thousands, or even tens of thousands, of people with M.B.A.s from the nation's best business schools and then filter out the ones who were best qualified and most interested in a particular job that a company needed to fill? "The breakthrough we had was to flip the model entirely," says Hyman. "Instead of having the whole thing be employer-centric and job-centric, why couldn't it be candidate-centric?" Hyman and Yuen designed a searchable database to store all the candidates' data and began to charge companies for access. Then they built a proprietary search engine to fish out the most qualified people according to each company's specifications and an e-mail system to contact those candidates to see if they were interested.

THE "-EST" CRAZE

Even if you lack some hard-core industry smarts in a particular area, it's still possible to get a decent business off the ground. After all, while the partners at Wet Feet Press and Career Central for MBAs knew the needs of their market pretty well, none of them had ever run a publishing company or a recruiting firm before. As they learned, if you can take an ordinary business and insert some truly unique idea or product into it, that's often all it takes. Take the restaurant business, by all accounts one of the toughest ones around no matter how old you are—how much could you increase your chances of survival if you offered people something they had never tasted before?

In 1991, Dave Hirschkop was 23 years old and selling burritos at a place he owned called Burrito Madness. When he opened it up, he did a lot of things right. For instance, he was serving wraps a long time before anyone else had thought of them, with burrito fillings like barbecued chicken and cajun shrimp. He also had the good sense to set up shop in College Park, Maryland, home of the state university and 30,000 students.

Still, his location wasn't perfect, and there were a couple of burrito shops more convenient to campus. Like all food service businesses in college towns, rowdy behavior posed some problems as well. "We had a lot of drunk customers who would come in really late at night and give us a hard time," Hirschkop recalls. How could he settle them down and get them out the door? "I figured if I gave them something really hot, they'd either sit there in pain quietly or leave quickly. Either one was good for me, and the hotter it was, the faster they'd be out of my hair.

"These guys were tough, macho guys, so when they would come in we would bait them. We'd ask them whether they wanted hot or mild sauce on their burrito, and if you're low-key enough about it, eventually they'll make some arrogant statement and ask for the hottest thing you've got. We'd only give it to them if they asked like that, and it was basically a license to kill.

"We made all our own sauces there, and by then, making hotter and hotter sauces had become a curiosity for me. Habaneros are the hottest peppers on earth, but habanero sauce had been done before. So I began thinking about making the hottest sauce on earth, extracting the essence of the pepper that makes it spicy and just putting that in the sauce. What would happen?"

As drunk people emerged from Burrito Madness reeling from the heat, desperate for water, and vomiting up the keg beer they had consumed that evening, Dave began to develop something of a reputation. People started showing up at Burrito Madness and actually asking for the stuff. So he bottled his spicy elixir and named it Dave's Insanity Sauce, then took it to the National Fiery Foods Show to see if he could sell some on a bigger stage.

"We went in trying to be gentle, diluting it into Bloody Mary mix," Dave recalls. "But we weren't making much of an impression. I finally decided that I wasn't going to be nice. I was going to hurt people. Otherwise, they'd take a taste and decide that there was nothing special about the product. It helped that I was wearing a straightjacket too, but once we served the product on its own, lines started forming and people were raving."

That is, until the law caught up with Dave. The sauce was so hot that someone panicked and called an ambulance when one show attendee consumed a bit too much and had trouble breathing. The show organizers told Dave that he couldn't serve the sauce anymore, making him the only purveyor ever to have a product banned from the Fiery Foods Show because it was too hot. As you might imagine, as a result of all the hysteria, a lot of merchants at the show heard about Dave and had to have his sauce in their stores. A few months later, he sold the burrito shop to concentrate on bottling his sauce.

As Hirschkop's experience suggests, taking things to extremes can have great rewards. In fact, extremism is one of those cultural trends worth noting, as it's popped up everywhere recently, from food (the hot sauce craze, the return of the steakhouse with brontosaurus-size cuts of meat) to athletics (extreme games, ultramarathons). Call it the "-est" craze—if you can serve the hottest or build the biggest, you'll create a lot of attention for yourself, if nothing else.

Chris and Pam Schmick learned this through pure serendipity. When the two met, Pam owned a dog-grooming business while Chris worked as a boilermaker using the metalworking skills he had picked up in the army. A rock-climbing nut, Chris soon turned Pam on to the sport, and they scraped together some money to buy a racquetball club that also had a small climbing wall. The club was in Peru, Illinois, a small town about 75 miles southwest of Chicago, but the couple purchased it with the intention of moving it. While they were thinking about heading to Chicago, tops on their list were nearby college towns in central Illinois.

"Most climbing gyms are built into old warehouse spaces," Chris explains. "But out in the middle of nowhere, warehouse space isn't very tall. Nobody needs to build up into the air there, since there's always a lot of space on either side of you." The couple had put a bunch of real estate brokers on to the case, but months went by with no one turning up any space that would work.

Frustrations were mounting. "Around here, you look around for something tall but then discover that it's taken," Chris says. As the couple was getting ready to give up, however, Chris happened to notice some abandoned grain silos on the outskirts of Bloomington, Illinois. "Using farm silos had never crossed my mind. They were just so big, so tall, that it had never occurred to either of us that they could work.

"But it was empty, and we began to dig deeper to see who

owned it. It turns out that it was kind of a heartbreak story. They were grain elevators that used to belong to a large seed company that had been bought out. The company had sold the land underneath to an excavator who was getting ready to tear the silos down. When we went in to see it, I knew immediately that it could work. It was nasty and disgusting inside from years of not having been cleaned out, but I could see what it would look like once it was." What resulted was Upper Limits, the world's largest indoor rock-climbing gym. Within a year of opening, the couple had been featured in *Sports Illustrated* and on several national television shows.

So we've seen the hottest and biggest, but what about the nicest? Customers care about how you treat them, and in the world of art galleries, there's traditionally been a premium placed on snottiness. Walking into most galleries is pretty intimidating; employees ignore you, yet there are no prices on any of the works, so they're the only ones who can help you navigate the place. If you're young and just beginning to think about starting to collect, you'd be hard-pressed to imagine an environment that's any less friendly.

Enter Elizabeth Burke, an artist herself, and her partner, Abby Messitte, whom you'll remember from the first chapter as the woman who couldn't cut it as a dictation-taking, dry-cleaning-fetching gallery assistant. At first, Burke had teamed up with a different partner, and their vision was utterly grandiose. " 'MTV goes fine art' was the original idea," says Burke. "Technically, it would be an art store, where you could walk off the street into a really funky atmosphere and just buy things off the walls." When it became clear how much it would cost to create a mega-retail space anywhere near New York City, Burke hooked up with Messitte and hit on the concept of an artist and customer-friendly smaller gallery.

"There were plenty of great artists that were shown only in nonprofit spaces in shows that they shared with 10 or 15 others," Burke says. "And then there were these disenfranchised people with extra income who would love to be able to own some art and be comfortable when they walked into a gallery to buy it." Adds Messitte: "We sort of thought of ourselves as members of our target audience, making the transition from having a college room to our own apartment. When you start to make money, you want to decorate with something other than framed posters, but my own experience had been that I needed to hound people at galleries to take the time to sell me something small."

THE RANDOM INVENTOR

Thanks to their friendly approach, the owners of Clementine have created an altogether different sort of gallery. Still, no matter how unique you are, it's never easy to start a business when you're competing against older, richer people who sell the same things you do. Obviously, if you can do something utterly new, your business will rise and fall simply on the merits of your product and how well you market it. Being truly original is a very tough task, as it's somewhat akin to trying to predict where lightning will strike. Still, plenty of young entrepreneurs have pulled it off with aplomb.

After years of hard work, a Minneapolis guitarist named Dave Kapell finally got his big break in 1993, but it wasn't a debut album that lifted him from obscurity—instead, it was a quirky habit that led to a booming business. Kapell entered his teenage years in

Minneapolis at a time when music was everywhere in town. Kapell dropped out of college, played in funk and heavy metal bands, and even did some acting as an extra in "Purple Rain." An avid songwriter, he was always looking for new ways to inspire himself lyrically, and he soon settled on a technique he had picked up watching a documentary about David Bowie.

"I made a habit of cutting up magazine stories, journal entries, letters from my sister—whatever interesting pieces of writing I could find—and rearranging the words to try and spark inspiration for songs," he recalls. "I wrote a song called 'Sailing North Dakota' that way. As a kid I learned to sail, and later on I would deliver cars around the U.S. just to travel, so those two things got combined through that method to describe what it's like to drive across the Dakotas at night. You can imagine you're on a narrow strip surrounded by water, just because it's so flat."

Kapell's bands did well locally, but he was far from being able to quit his various day jobs doing clerical work for a variety of nonprofits. Still, he kept at it in his kitchen in the evenings, trying to dream up the next great song. "The problem was, I had allergies," he recalls. "So I would have this great poem laid out, and then I would sneeze and the wind from the sneeze would send these bits of paper with the words on them flying all over the place. I thought about gluing all the words to cardboard so they would be heavier, but then I would have to put all of them away in a box and then take them all out again every time I wanted to use them.

"One of my roommates at the time worked at a pizza place, and they had a huge batch of reject refrigerator magnet advertisements that had been made with misprints. She brought them home for me figuring I'd find some use for them, and I realized I could glue the words to the magnets and then stick them on a metal cookie sheet. That way, I wouldn't have to put all these hundreds of words away all the time."

If Kapell hadn't been short on cash at the time, he probably would have gone out and bought a bunch of cookie sheets. Since that didn't seem like a great way to spend his money, however, the house went cookieless for a while. "Finally, one day someone really wanted to make cookies, and I had to figure out what to do with all these words," he recalls. "We just did the logical thing since they were made from refrigerator magnets and stuck them up there."

Almost immediately, pandemonium struck in that kitchen in Minneapolis. "Suddenly, every one of my roommates seemed to be gathering around the fridge laughing and playing with this thing," he says. "The same thing happened when we had parties. There were all these grotesque and bizarre words. I remember one that my roommate Cory wrote: 'I stared as Alan fingered his cancer.' People would make suggestions for new words to use and give me other ideas, like adding more 'ly' magnets to make adverbs."

Even Kapell, who had never actively sought to start a business at all, realized that a great product, Magnetic Poetry, had been born. "People started asking for them, and I told everyone that I could make one for seven bucks," he says. "I was making seven dollars an hour at my job at the time and my student loans were coming due, so I made up a bunch of kits. I took 100 to the first craft show I went to, figuring that would be enough for the whole weekend. They sold out in three hours."

Dave Kapell's little invention was so ingenious that it probably would have been a hit at any moment in recent history. Other start-ups are more time sensitive, since when a new medium, like the Internet, is born, those who plant their flags in a particular area first have an opportunity to build a brand name for themselves before anyone else gets there. Amazon.com is a perfect example, as it was online long before Barnes and Noble got there.

Even before Amazon made its appearance, however, there was another retail innovator in cyberspace. Over drinks in a bar one night, Jason Olim, a young programmer who worked for a consulting firm, came up with the idea for an online record store. Really, it sounds clichéd, but a lot of great businesses are born over beer. "It was just like, boom, there it was," he recalls. It was early 1994, a few months before people began to use the Web widely but long after millions of potential customers had gone online through a university Internet server or by using commercial online services like America Online. "My friends and I talked about it the whole time we were at the bar. And by the next day, I had already started. I was writing to the online services, looking for suppliers, and searching for how-to-start-your-business books."

Olim did have some music in his past. He had played a fair bit of guitar and had done sound at Brown, where he went to college. And like Clementine's Abby Messitte, Olim had also been disappointed with his experiences as a shopper. "At the time I started the business, I vividly remembered being in college, discovering Miles Davis's 'Kind of Blue,' and going to the record store to seek out some more of his music," he recalls. "I was in this Tower Records in Boston, which at the time it opened was supposed to be the biggest, best record store on the planet. So I go to the jazz section and ask the guy for a recommendation on the next Miles Davis album I should buy. He has no idea. What a fucking idiot. He just says that they're all good. So I buy 'Bitches Brew,' and I challenge anyone to hum a melody from the album. It took me years to listen to that all the way through, and I still don't really like it all that much.

"So I started going to the record store with books in hand, things that offered up recommendations for me since no one at the record stores ever could. The books weren't really complete enough, but they were all right." But what if he could put all that information online, so that you could read reviews of every album, in every genre? What if you could click your mouse and hear tracks off the album? If you could, Olim figured, his business, CD-Now, could make Tower Records a thing of the past.

Obviously, Olim's timing couldn't have been better. His only obstacle was executing his vision, since there was little in the way of real competition online at that point. Still, that's not to say that there aren't some good retail opportunities left on the Net. No one's built a database of specialty food sellers. Grocery-shopping services still are not widespread. There isn't a decent site for sporting goods or for used musical instruments. You get the idea.

But the biggest online opportunity of all is in community building. By now, you've probably gagged listening to all the jabbering about virtual communities as the new town centers of American life. It sounds like a lot of theoretical mumbo-jumbo, but upstarts have built great businesses just by giving people a place where they can talk to one another about particular topics.

Take the Gardner brothers and their Motley Fool personal finance site that started on America Online. "What really drove us was a conscious effort not to be the experts, not to have all the answers," David explains. "We didn't know a lot about the oil industry, but there was this guy out in Houston who had worked in it, so he would log on and answer people's questions about particular issues or companies whose stock they were thinking about buying. It was, in retrospect, the total new media model, which is just to celebrate the people. These people are great and interesting and they aren't being quoted in the newspapers or on television. But here they all are online, and we can harness them there and deliver them to one another." Where else had any of those people ever had an opportunity like that before, to debate ideas back and forth with thousands of others who were passionately interested in investing, just like they were? Certainly not in *Money* magazine, or on the Louis Rukeyser show that David Gardner had been affiliated with.

GRAND THEFT START-UP

OK, so not everyone has the vision or the technical know-how to build a winning business in an entirely new medium like the Internet. Maybe you're not as creative as Dave Kapell, with his magnetic poetry kits. Or perhaps you can't think of any new twist on the ice cream parlor or the video game. Think you're doomed to entrepreneurial failure? One of the most overlooked entrepreneurial strategies, and perhaps the best one of all, is simply to steal. There are millions of great businesses in the world, but none of them reach every customer they can. So if you've heard about a great business idea and no one is using it where you are, there's no crime in simply stealing it and putting it to work yourself.

Tom Baron and Juno Yoon didn't get their start in the restaurant business at Mad Mex. In fact, they had another restaurant handed to them on a silver platter. The two high school friends had moved to San Francisco in their mid-20s, but their lives changed entirely when Yoon got a phone call from his mother one day. "I come from a fairly traditional Korean family, and since I was the eldest son, my parents weren't incredibly happy that I had left home," he explains. "My mom had always had an entrepreneurial spirit, but she stayed at home with us because that's just the way it was back then. But she had gotten bored, and when she called that day it was to tell me that she'd bought a restaurant from a friend. She wanted me to come back and run it. I thought the whole thing was a great idea. I would get to be my own boss at age 21. Not that I knew how to run a restaurant or anything."

Yoon returned to New York and eventually convinced Baron to come back and help him. Turns out that Yoon's mother had bought into a coffee shop with a standard breakfast and lunch menu, a classic Manhattan establishment that seemed to be on every street corner in the 1980s. With so many of those places around, it was always a wonder how they all survived.

Yoon and Baron soon learned what a struggle it was. "We didn't have air conditioning in the middle of the summer for a long time," Baron recalls. "We were just amazed that any customers came in at all. I honestly think people came in just because it was entertaining to watch us work. It was pathetic how bad it was. Our record was serving three bugs to one person in one meal. After the third one, the one in her coffee, she finally walked out.

"Just to explain how immature we were, we got this incredible deal on these to-go cups. They were specimen cups, urine specimen cups. You can imagine what kind of reaction you might get if you were serving apple juice in one of those. I remember this person calling and just screaming at us . . . while Juno and I cracked up. We realized that this venture wasn't going anywhere, and I left Juno to deal with the sinking ship." Juno managed to avoid paying rent the final few months by pretending he didn't speak English, but the coffee shop ultimately closed.

Baron ended up moving to Pittsburgh and lived with his sister, and the food service bug quickly caught up with him. At the time, you couldn't get home delivery there for anything except pizza, so he found a partner and started a business to pick food up at restaurants and deliver it to people's homes. The partners did fine, but after a few years Baron was itching to build something bigger, so he began to look for something else to do.

That's when *Pittsburgh* magazine came out with its annual "Best Of" issue. Baron leafed through it, and one thing in particular caught his eye: Chi-Chi's, a national chain, had won the honors for the city's best Mexican restaurant. "It was just ridiculous that Chi-Chi's was the best that this town had to offer," Baron recalls. "Juno had done the smart thing and gone out west to be a ski bum after the coffee shop closed, and I called him up and told him that we had a golden opportunity."

Juno got the call and immediately knew that this was the idea they had been waiting for. "Having lived in California and eaten a lot of good tacos there, we both knew how bad Chi-Chi's food was. It couldn't be that hard to be better than they were."

While California taco and burrito shops offered the culinary template for what the pair could offer in Pittsburgh, they planned to crib some concepts from the restaurant scene in New York City as well. "At the time, in the late '80s and early '90s, there were so many fun Mexican restaurants in New York City," Baron recalls. "These were true bar-restaurants, where you could eat or drink and have a great time. In Pittsburgh, you ate first and went to the bar afterwards, or just went to the bar. There was nothing wild going on in Pittsburgh at all."

Though Pittsburgh is a fairly conservative town, Baron and Yoon knew that in the right area, their restaurant concept, Mad

Mex, could work. They picked a spot near the University of Pittsburgh, made it look cool without spending a fortune, and flung open the doors. "We were not afraid to turn up the stereo and have a funky wait staff," Baron says. "It was definitely a party every night we were open." Though the two fully admit that their restaurant management skills left a lot to be desired at the time, it didn't matter. People were waiting two hours to get in every night, because they'd never seen anything like it in Pittsburgh before.

Restaurants and other retail storefront operations make great businesses, since you can take someone else's idea and simply bring it someplace new. But just because you're a manufacturer of products that get sold at those stores doesn't mean that you can't do well too. You just have to take a product that's already out there and make it better.

For at least two decades, lots of people have preached the principles of environmentally sensitive management, using recycled materials to make products that don't harm the earth. It's a noble idea, but few companies have made it work, since most products made from recycled goods just don't look very good. And when they don't look good, they're generally not profitable because nobody wants to buy them. Rob Brandagee knew all about this, but it didn't faze him. His parents had run their own company, and he figured that his experiences bouncing around North America waiting tables, teaching people to ski, and running a hot dog cart were only short diversions from his path to owning his own business. "My parents had done it for a long time, so I just saw no reason why I couldn't do the same thing," he says.

"I had seen this company on the West Coast. They were making bags and things with recycled materials, and it seemed like a pretty neat idea, but it kind of had that crunchy granola stigma.

Their stuff wasn't high quality, the design wasn't great, and they just didn't tell their story in the same way that I would have."

As Brandagee's idea was taking shape, he became involved romantically with Ava DeMarco, a graphic designer who lived near him in Pittsburgh. "My dad had a shop down in the basement and he liked to work on cars, so I was always into mechanical and structural things like that," she says. "But I grew up in West Virginia, so I also learned to appreciate the environment. My mom used to take us on nature hikes to see the copperhead snakes and pick flowers."

DeMarco majored in graphic design at college, learning a lot about packaging and product design along the way, and was a partner in a design firm for several years before she met Brandagee. "By that point, I had it all worked out in my head," Brandagee said. "The business was going to be a cross between The Body Shop and Ben and Jerry's. We wanted to be product-driven, the way Ben and Jerry are with their ice cream. But we also wanted to use materials from all over the world, creating mini-economies for the recycled materials we would need in the same way that Ben and Jerry and The Body Shop do for their own raw materials."

With DeMarco working with him on the weekends to execute his far-flung ideas, the two came up with their first few products. One was a belt made from recycled tire inner tubes and decorated with old bottle caps that they scavenged from bars. The second was a backpack made from similar rubber festooned with colorful old license plates from various states. They christened the company Little Earth and produced a few samples.

Since their stuff was essentially made from trash, raw material costs were low. And because labor is free when you're making your products on the dining room table, profitability seemed like it was within the couple's grasp. Like Kapell, they tried their luck at a craft show, and by the end of their second one, they had booked over $30,000 in orders. "Which led us to our next problem," DeMarco recalled. "We had sold all these products, but they didn't exist in real life yet. How and where were we going to make all these things?"

We'll get there in another few chapters but we're not done with the thievery yet. We've established that you can bring New York and California to middle America, but what about Europe? Before Nantucket Nectars was born, Tom Scott and Tom First were delivering supplies to yachts in Nantucket Harbor in Massachusetts. But it wasn't one of their customers who demanded bottled juice along with the daily papers, bread, and toilet paper that the partners dropped off each day. "It all started because I had been to Spain in 1989 to visit a girlfriend and had tried this peach nectar that you drank out of a bottle," First recalls. "It wasn't sugary, like most of the juice in the States at the time. You could tell that there was actual juice in there. I had tried making it in a blender when I came back, but it wasn't until two years later, when we were looking for something to do that wasn't as seasonal as the boat business that we actually decided to try to bottle it."

Then there's Amy Nye Wolf, whose idea had been dormant even longer than First's. "When I was 17, I took a trip to Europe for a few weeks before I started college," she recalls. "By the time I came back through Heathrow Airport in London, I had listened to all the tapes I had brought for my Walkman many times over. There was this little cart full of tapes at the airport. The selection was lousy and the prices were twice what they were in the record store, but I still bought some. At the time, there was really no shopping to speak of in U.S. airports, especially if you wanted music.

"So I tucked that away while I went to college and during my time working as an analyst at Goldman Sachs. I took a lot of day trips for Goldman, so I spent a lot of time waiting for late flights. By then, I had a Discman, but I still couldn't do any music shopping in U.S. airports. Originally, I thought I was going to start an educational software company, and I remember walking down the street one day looking at the squares on the sidewalk and thinking about computers. And all of the sudden, it occurred to me that that cart in Heathrow could fit in a couple of those squares. How much could it cost to launch something like that? That's where it all started."

Sure, it helps to be a brilliant visionary. Jason Olim's notion of a vastly improved shopping experience has raised the bar for every record retailer in the world. But if you're looking for a great business idea, it's even more important to have a good set of eyes and ears. Tower Records and HMV had undoubtedly looked at airport space before, but no one had thought to set up kiosks, just like they do in Europe. The concept Amy Nye Wolf copied and brought to the United States is now in over 20 airports.

CHAPTER 3

IN SEARCH OF CUSTOMERS

A Quick Primer on Market Research

By the time you've lived with your great idea for a couple days, you'll probably be way ahead of yourself. You'll be thinking about how to decorate your office or store, what your ads will say, and what your business cards will look like. It's all important stuff, to be sure. But before you dive into any of that, it's important to do a bit of homework just to make sure that this business of yours is really going to fly.

"One of the things my father instilled in me when I went to him for help was to always ask the following questions," says Altitunes's Amy Nye Wolf. "Why hasn't anybody done this before, and why can't they copy you once you do it?" Along with the obvious question about where to find customers comes these two fundamental issues that Wolf's dad fixes on. The first one revolves around figuring out which industry you're actually going to be operating in and getting a sense of its history. The second one assumes that you're entering a market where there isn't much competition. If that's the case, why is that? Did they already die a few years ago after attempting to execute the same stupid idea that you just stumbled on? You'd better hope not, and doing some good, old-fashioned market research is the best way to figure all this out.

BACK TO THE LIBRARY

First, the industry research. Doug Chu and Scott Samet spent their first two years out of the University of Pennsylvania working as analysts in Los Angeles for Bankers Trust, an investment bank. Then the entrepreneurial bug bit, and their idea was to sell healthy snacks in movie theaters and call it Taste of Nature. While their banking experience hadn't prepared them for dealing with theater owners, it taught them how to crash a research project. "You've got to look at all the major components of the business at the beginning," says Samet. "How do you get your product? Where do you go to figure out who makes the best product? We went to grocery stores and convenience stores to find out what people were buying both from bulk bins and in packaging and what price they seemed to be willing to pay for it. Once we knew we could provide things that people would actually buy, we had to figure out if we could display it, since counter space is at a premium in movie theaters."

Had they noticed this space crunch during their visits to movie theaters over the years? Hardly. They simply went to the people who ran the theaters before they started building counter displays and asked. "In a centralized industry like this one, where there are a few really big chains of movie theaters, the universe of people we needed to contact was actually pretty small," Chu says. "There were people who ran concessions for each of the chains, maybe 10 or 20 in all, and we were able to meet with half of them." Those folks at the chains told them about another resource as well, the National Association of Theater Operators. Like all industry associations (and every industry has one), this one was happy to turn over a wealth of useful information to the partners.

Another thing you'll find in almost every sizable industry is a consultant or other expert who has already gone out and tracked down every last bit of information you could ever want. Most directors of industry associations will be able to tell you who these people are. In the movie theater business, they know how many people visit movie theaters each year, how often they tend to go, and what they spend their money on at the concession stands. The Taste of Nature partners learned that there were no healthy items being sold in movie theaters at all, and that the total take from movie concessions in the year before they launched the business was about $4 billion. What if they could get just 1 percent of that? Sometimes this data will show up in industry trade journals, or an association might have it handy. If you can't get it for free, however, be prepared to spend at least a couple hundred dollars buying it from someone else, since there's probably no way you can run all this stuff down on your own.

Amy Nye Wolf, who wanted to sell compact discs in airports, had higher hurdles to clear because she was trying to extract data from the government officials who control most airports. For decades, no one was able to buy anything useful at airport stores, the bad food cost twice as much as it would have someplace else, and there was a simple reason why. Until the mid-1990s, city and state airport authorities were either corrupt, incompetent, or both, concerned mostly with paying off the unions that represented airport workers and wooing the airlines that used the facilities. Airline passengers and their shopping needs were pretty low on the priority list, and the overarching bureaucracy scared potential merchants away.

So Amy Nye Wolf approached her research with no small amount of trepidation. She first called the Port Authority, which is the agency that runs the three airports in New York. "After getting transferred around to at least 15 guys, I finally found someone who sounded pretty young and seemed like he understood what I was trying to do." Not a bad strategy, as a young person on the up-and-up at any big organization is likely to get what you're trying to do and help you out. Not only was the man Wolf found willing to help, but it turned out that she had entered this market at exactly the right moment. The people who ran the airports were finally paying attention to the passengers who used their facilities. Why? Enlightened self-interest basically, for they got wise to how well their agencies could do if they took a cut of every merchant's sales instead of asking them to pay a fixed rent. The airport official brought Wolf in for a meeting, and negotiations proceeded from there.

Previous work experience can help here, for if you've worked in a particular industry before, you'll already have a lot of the knowledge you need. This can happen one of two ways. First, your idea for a new business will come as a result of all your previous work. Elizabeth Burke and Abby Messitte had seen enough of the snooty New York art world to know that a kinder, gentler approach to running a gallery might work wonders. Robert Stephens knew that the Geek Squad would fly in part because of all the people that seemed to need his help with their home computers. But he also was working in a computer lab at the University of Minnesota at the time, so he could see trends in the computer industry changing. "First, CompUSA and places like that were opening up, selling computers to the masses," he said. "Then, modems started getting cheaper, which enabled the Internet to really take off because people could log on from their homes. What if there was one person you could call for everything from help on your Mac or PC to replacing your power supply when it goes down at 11 P.M. and you've got a trade show the next morning?"

The second way to go at this is to dream up your idea and then work in that industry to get some experience before you start your company. Most restaurateurs start out this way, as Tom Baron and Juno Yoon of Mad Mex did. But it's a useful tactic in almost any industry, even if it's not in the exact area you intend to work in once you're running your own show. Before Malia Mills started her swimwear company with Julia Stern, she worked at a department store and for the designer Jessica McClintock, who had gotten her own start as a young entrepreneur designing alternative wedding dresses for hippies in the San Francisco Bay area. "I would have never worn any of her clothes," Mills says. "But if I had just been working for Calvin Klein or something, it wouldn't have forced me to think. I had to figure out what worked about her clothes, why people spent a lot of money on some things but not others, and what it was about her image that caused mobs to form when she made appearances at department stores." Along with all that higher-order thinking, Mills also picked up a lot of nuts-and-bolts knowledge about how things get sold and delivered to those stores in the first place.

EXCUSE ME, BUT WOULD YOU BUY MY PRODUCT?

Once you know a little bit more about your industry, it's time to start figuring out who your potential customers actually are, what they might want to buy, and how much they'd be willing to spend to buy it from you. This isn't rocket science, though it's not an exact science either. It's true that market research generally involves nothing more than the kind of data gathering the Taste of Nature guys did, plus some actual surveys of individual consumers. The reason it's not always a completely accurate portrayal of how people behave is that they lie about what they'll actually buy once you have something real to offer them. Some people simply can't bring themselves to disappoint an eager young upstart brandishing a questionnaire. That's no reason not to interview a bunch of potential customers—just don't base your financial projections solely on what they tell you they'd be willing to spend once you're in business.

There's a couple ways to go at this. The first is pretty basic—just find some people who fit in the demographic group you're trying to hit and have them answer a few questions. One way to do this is with a simple written survey asking people what they need, what they'd be willing to try, and how much they'd spend to try it. Chris and Pam Schmick polled students at Illinois State University about their rock-climbing habits and also spread the survey around corporate headquarters at nearby State Farm Insurance. "We asked them if they had ever climbed before, where, if they'd be interested in learning, how much they'd be willing to pay, how often they would come, all those sorts of things," Pam recalls. "We also asked them what radio stations they listened to so we'd have a better idea of where we might advertise."

Though the Schmicks found mostly what they expected—which was a lot of interest in rock climbing—some companies discover that their ideas about what customers need are way off base. That's what happened to Career Central for MBAs, and surveys helped correct it. "We thought what people needed was software that you'd buy in a store that would help you with your résumé and then have a database of contacts that you could send it to," Hyman recalls. "That was too software-focused and not candidate-focused enough. What the surveys showed was that people in business school knew how to write their résumés already. They didn't need help with that. They wanted fresh job leads tailored to their interests. So we decided to give the software away to the candidates and sell our service, which was the access to those candidates, to the employers.

"It's hard to realize right off the bat that your concept sucks," he adds. "The temptation is to talk first to your friends and other people who know you. They're worthless, because they don't want to discourage you, so they won't tell you anything that you don't want to hear. So we faxed our surveys out to everyone we knew and asked them to fax it out to ten more people. The response rate wasn't great, but we learned enough to know where we had gone wrong."

You can also put together a focus group, where you entice a dozen or so people into a room for an hour or two with some free food and then let them bounce their answers to your questions off one another. "The first one was a collection of people who were more connected with the art world," says Clementine art gallery's

Abby Messitte. "Later on, we did a more serious group of people that we didn't know. They were all young professionals, and, thankfully, they all felt the same way as we did about the way art was marketed. Some of them even became clients, which was very nice."

The other way to poll your target audience is a lot like the first method, except it's slightly more aggressive. This one involves going out and finding your customers in the particular place you'd like to set up shop and accosting them there. "I did a two-page questionnaire and went to the airport to hand it out to people who were waiting for flights," says Altitunes's Amy Nye Wolf. "People were fairly cooperative, since they're all bored at the airport. The positive response rate was 80 percent, so they seemed pretty psyched about it. While you can't count them all as customers, it was a pretty good sign that I was on to something."

It also helps to get at potential customers when they're in the right mental frame of mind. The partners behind Wet Feet Press, the insider guides to life at various companies, first tested their products on people at Stanford who were coming out of those drippy presentations that corporations make when they come to schools to do on-campus recruiting. "We would stand outside the restaurants where the companies made their pitches and hand out flyers," says Wet Feet cofounder Gary Alpert. "And then the next day, we'd start getting calls. 'Well, Gemini Consulting is interesting, but what I'd really like is McKinsey.' So we'd just race to put a McKinsey report together before they came to campus."

As Alpert suggests, one of the best ways to begin to put your market research to work is to test out a few products on the survey subjects who have said they would want them. "One of the best ways to start a business on a conservative budget is to use the peek-in," explains Taste of Nature's Doug Chu. "Instead of spending a lot of money to make a big bet, peek in to the potential of a particular market or product by placing a small ad instead of a big one or doing a modest production run of a particular item, just to see how it sells." Adds Little Earth's Ava DeMarco: "Test marketing in stores is a lot different than having people sitting around a table telling you whether or not they'd actually buy something."

Though he wasn't conscious of it at the time, this was the approach that Todd Alexander ended up using for his first big wine order for Vendemmia, his wine distributorship in Atlanta. "My first order was for one container, which is 1,000 cases," he recalls. "These were wines that compared very well with their peer group from Italy in terms of price but that didn't necessarily have anything to do with their marketability. For years, people in Atlanta drank white zinfandel, Jack Daniels, and Budweiser. You can't come in with esoteric Italian wines when people are only a few years past Bud." The retailers he sold to, mainly wine and liquor stores and restaurants, knew this already and didn't want a lot of his wine.

The problem was, Alexander hadn't exactly figured that out before he had those first 1,000 cases shipped over from Italy. "I ended up drinking a lot of my wine in 1994," he notes sheepishly, recalling how he adjusted his second order to better reflect the needs of his market. "It's a costly error, but you can always try to sell it all for what you paid for it and call it a wash. You've lost some opportunity costs, but at least wine is a tangible asset that you can liquidate" (or simply consume on your own).

EXCUSE ME, BUT WOULD YOU SELL MY PRODUCT?

Though Alexander did get to do a lot of great drinking during his first year in business, he might have learned his lesson more cheaply if there had been a trade show for Georgia wine sellers. That way, he could have seen if the real experts—the merchants who were actually going to sell his wares—thought his products would sell. Trade shows are also good for simply getting noticed. Dave Hirschkop capitalized on this in a huge way when his product was booted from the Fiery Foods Show because it was too hot. While the results don't have to be quite so dramatic to prove that you have a winner on your hands, it does help to draw attention to yourself.

"We spent a lot of time before the first show thinking about how we were going to make a really cool impression," recalls Little Earth's Rob Brandagee. "We took some of our products, went to a junkyard with some friends, took some really clean, high-end photos of them carrying the products, and just put those on the table at our booth." Oh, and then there were the cutoffs and the little bathing suit tops that his partner, Ava (now his wife), used to wear. "We've toned it down a bit since then," she says. But it was enough to draw traffic at the beginning, given that both of them are good-looking enough to be models themselves. With $30,000 in orders from their first show, they had enough confidence to produce a whole line of bags.

You don't have to be gorgeous to succeed at a trade show, of course. But you do have to get a spot in the first place. At one particularly important show, Brandagee and DeMarco had to illegally sublet a booth from another purveyor just to get themselves in. And when Kate and Andy Space hit their first big New York accessories show, they just barely got in, and the only spots left were near the hot dog stand. "The people with seniority get the better space, even though you don't pay less for bad space," Andy explains. "But the great thing is, the fashion editors who can break a product like ours out are like people in flea markets; they're always looking around in corners for the next great find. And that's how the woman from Barney's found us." While the Barney's order wasn't enough to make the business profitable, the store is a major trendsetter, so its endorsement was a sign to others that the Kate Spade bags were worth a careful look.

The other great thing about trade shows is that they make it convenient to size up the competition. Since almost every company in every industry heads to several of these things each year, it's open season on spying. By checking everyone else out, your own vision of the niche you'll fill will probably crystallize. "There was very little out there that was truly timeless, the kind of thing that you knew would be available year after year," Kate Spade says, echoing the inklings that led her to start her handbag company in the first place. "I see it in my own life now. If I found a great pair of pants, I'd love to know that I could buy them season after season in all different fabrics. But you can't. So now when I find a great pair of shoes, I'll buy two or three pairs because I know that with only one, I'd wear them out and then not be able to find the same pair again." Now at least she doesn't have to do that with her handbags.

If you're planning on offering a service, the only way to do similar research is to go out and experience the competition yourself. "I'd gone for quite a few facials all over New York City just to see what other people were doing," says Marcia Kilgore of Bliss. "Too many of them were just doing the tsk-tsk hard-ass sort of thing, scolding you for having blackheads. You don't really need shit from your facialist. But I remember one time in particular when I was going to treat myself to a facial after I finished an economics exam for a course I was taking. I'd been to this place once before, and they had sold me a bunch of products that hadn't done anything to improve my skin. So the facialist takes one look at me and says, 'Uch, you could have such nice skin if you took better care of it.' Then he goes and gets the owner, and they proceed to try and sell me all the same things they had sold me there last time.

"So there I was having looked forward to this treat all week long. I really wanted to have fun and relax and get my skin cleaned out, and they're embarrassing me. That's no way to treat a customer. It doesn't make you want to go back. It makes you want to hide, which is what you're always trying to do if you have bad skin in the first place. They're supposed to be professionals, and there they are making fun of you. I realized that that was definitely not the way to go." Indeed, a little empathy can clearly go a long way in business. While Kilgore does see a lot of models with picture-perfect skin at Bliss, to this day she still enjoys working with people with problem complexions more than anything else.

As Kilgore's experience suggests, how you deliver something has as much to do with its success as the strength of your product or service itself. Malia Mills learned this lesson by watching what was new in the fashion magazines that reported on the swimwear shows and noting the problems with the way suits were sold. "Buying swimwear has always been a totally unpleasant experience, because you couldn't buy a top and bottom in different sizes," she says. "I read a lot about lingerie before starting the company, and the logic there, where you could buy any bra in any fabric, size, or color, and match it with any bottom according to fit, activity, and mood, well, why didn't it make sense for swimwear too?"

There were other problems with the swimwear market, similar to the gaps that Kate Spade had noticed. "The market was lacking in a certain taste level," Mills adds. "What Calvin Klein stands for in clothing, I wasn't seeing in swimsuits. There were the very fussy suits with lots of gold buttons and details, and then there was the very basic stuff from J Crew. There was room for something in between, with some sophistication and color but not anything that was totally over the top."

EXPECT THE UNEXPECTED

Once you think you have your market niche nailed down, don't worry if you think it looks too small. Opportunities to expand will present themselves in strange places, as they did for Kate Spade, who's now making bags for men too. And they did so for Malia Mills, who designed a flip-flop for another company and is looking to license her name for other deals.

Customers you never expected to cater to will come out of the woodwork too. At Wet Feet Press, the companies that were the subject of the insider guides started calling and buying hundreds of copies at once. "At first I think they just wanted to let people inside the company know what was being said about them, so they could be prepared to address the issues if someone asked about them during a job interview," cofounder Alpert says. "But then they realized that they would look pretty good by not hiding from what we were saying about them, and they began to distribute the guides themselves to niche groups that they hadn't been successful in recruiting from before." For instance, a consulting firm might send its Wet Feet guide to law students to entice them into their industry and keep them from joining a big corporate law firm.

At Altitunes, Amy Nye Wolf realized that there was a huge part of her market that she hadn't even noticed at first. "Airline employees became such good customers," she says. "It's as much as 20 percent of our sales in some locations." Turns out that flight attendants and pilots have long layovers, and many of them travel with portable compact disc players. Airport employees who work at the airport every day also started doing a lot of their music shopping with Altitunes.

Even competitors may turn out to be customers, which is what happened with Career Central for MBAs. Though their ability to do quick, targeted searches for companies looking for M.B.A.'s with a specific set of skills and experience undoubtedly takes business away from traditional headhunting firms, those firms are some of its best customers. "Two of the three top search firms already use us," notes Jeffrey Hyman. "They use us for particularly tough searches or for those that will net them a fee below what they usually work for but that they want to do anyway to please a big client." Because Career Central for MBAs charges about a tenth of what these firms stand to make for the search that Career Central is helping them with, Career Central's fee is practically a rounding error to the search firms. In the meantime, the firms can look like heroes to their clients, and Career Central lands another fee.

As this example suggests, there's no possible way to predict every place a customer might turn up. So perhaps if you're aiming to serve a demographic group that's roughly similar to your own, you may do fine by simply winging it. "We make what we feel like making," says Nantucket Nectars's Tom Scott. "It's more of a collective we now that the company is bigger, but it's still a gut feeling. You can feel what your stomach wants.

"We once went into a meeting with someone who had gotten hold of some market research data from Ocean Spray. She said that they had tested guava as a flavor and decided that the name evoked negative images for people. We looked at each other and said, 'OK, we're making it.' Now, it's one of our top sellers. So we learned that lesson.

"The thing about the world today—and maybe it's always been this way—is that it's moving really fast. It's easier and easier to get new things these days, because product information moves so much faster. Things like ginseng or juice bars, they happened so fast that market research couldn't have kept up. You have to be in the middle of it to understand it. That's why Tom and I have always been part of every major product decision that the company has made. Not because we're better or because we're smarter, but because we've been there the whole time. Juice is just part of our everyday reality now."

There's nothing wrong with this point of view, though the two Toms are definitely in the minority on this one. Admittedly, doing market research sounds a lot like pulling teeth. However, once you get started (if you get started), you'll see that it isn't. It's somewhat akin to doing homework, except this time it adds up to something more than just a grade on a transcript. It can lead you in a totally different, more profitable direction if you pick up on the right cues.

CHAPTER 4

CAN YOU GO IT ALONE?

The Ups and Downs of Having a Business Partner

Two heads are better than one." "No man is an island." The clichés promoting the virtues of partnership are seemingly endless. Small business owners in the United States seem to be split on the subject, with about half running companies in which only one person owns a majority stake while the other half work with at least one partner. But among young entrepreneurs, few go it alone. Although there are success stories like that of Michael Dell (of Dell Computers) and Jake Burton (of Burton Snowboards), most young people come to the conclusion that they don't have the knowledge or experience to do everything themselves on a daily basis.

"I can't understand how people do it on their own. The fact that we have completely different strengths makes it a lot easier to go the distance," notes Little Earth's Rob Brandagee, who creates bags, date books, and other accessories out of recycled products with his wife, Ava DeMarco. Adds Tom Scott, who started Nantucket Nectars with his college friend Tom First: "We share a certain drive, but we don't share the same personality traits or skills. He's more intense and diligent about particular things. He worries about whether we're using FedEx or UPS and will spend a lot of time on one small item in a contract with a distributor. But it's a damn good thing he's around, because I know that there are a lot of things that I just don't have to worry about."

SO WHAT SHOULD YOU LOOK FOR IN A PARTNER?

If you run through a list of your best friends, you'll probably come across many whom you truly care about but would undoubtedly drive you crazy if you had to work with them. Once you subtract that group, though, how can you tell which of the others might make good partners?

First of all, you have to trust your partner. "Tom is one in a million, and he's the only friend I could have done this with," says Nantucket Nectars's Tom Scott. "There's a certain selflessness, a sense of sharing, that's always been there with us from the beginning. We're firm believers in capitalism, but when we started out serving the boats in Nantucket Harbor it was like a communist enterprise. I had the towing license, so I'd earn $90 an hour to go out and rescue boats while Tom was delivering groceries. But at the end of the day, we'd sit down and divide it in equal parts. We actually sat and wrote it down at one point, that that was how things were going to work."

Scott makes it all out to be fairly nice and neat, but inevitably you and your partners are going to have some disagreements. What will it be like to argue with them? Will you be able to kiss and make up after some truly heated disagreements? By the time Tom Baron and Juno Yoon reached their late 20s, they had been friends since ninth grade, had been roommates in California, and had run a coffee shop together in New York City. So when they considered opening a Mexican restaurant in Pittsburgh, they already knew each other well enough to know that they had a decent working relationship. "Juno and I are from New York City, so we can be hot-headed and scream and yell at each other and no one is ever offended," says Baron. "We've learned that we have to tone it down a little bit when we're dealing with our employees. But for two partners, it's an ideal relationship because we always know exactly what the other one thinks. There's no holding back at all."

This kind of comfort level is something you build over a long period of time, and the partners at Mad Mex and Nantucket Nectars had been friends for years before they started their companies. But what if you're considering working with someone you aren't close friends with? It helps if you can see the glint in their eyes, something that can confirm your hunches about their work ethic and level of desire. Malia Mills and Julia Stern both went to Cornell and were friends as undergraduates, but they fell out of touch once they graduated. When Stern went to work as an editor on the *Sports Illustrated* swimsuit issue, though, she was constantly in search of innovative bathing suits. Remembering how intense Mills's work ethic was in college, Stern tracked her down and asked her to come up with some new designs.

"She'd be locked into the design studio all night at school and we would bring her breakfast the next morning," Stern recalls. "So

I knew that if I made the phone call to her, she'd act on it and I'd get a perfectly put-together FedEx package of suits right after that. I had respect for her design talent and work ethic, so I didn't think it would have mattered whether I'd asked her for bathing suits or coats." Mills launched a company based on her work for the magazine, and Stern eventually left to join her.

It's also crucial to work with people who make up for whatever deficiencies you have yourself. Jeffrey Hyman knew he didn't have the technical skills to start Career Central for MBAs on his own, so he did a lot of snooping around Silicon Valley before he turned up Lun Yuen just a few cubicles away from him at Intuit. "I was interviewing 30 people at Starbucks every weekend," Hyman says. "But that was like going on blind dates. I was never going to find anyone that way. Then I heard that Lun had been thinking about leaving Intuit too. So I asked around, and I heard incredible things about him." Yuen picked over Hyman's business plan and decided that it was worth a shot.

BUT SHOULD YOU WORK WITH YOUR LIFE PARTNER?

However risky teaming up with a friend may be, the potential for disaster is even greater when there's more than just a friendship at stake. It takes true courage to start a company with your significant other, and it also necessitates setting up some safeguards and establishing sound priorities. "We would never let the business destroy our relationship," says Kate Spade, who started her handbag company with her then-boyfriend, now-husband, Andy. Adds Andy: "What's the worst thing that could happen if it failed? We'd pay off whatever debts we had with our contractors and fabric people and I'd go back to working at an ad agency."

The Spades's attitude is a pretty healthy one as far as it goes. Still, bankruptcy isn't the only thing that leads to failed relationships, for the simple day-to-day stress of running your own company while spending 24 hours a day on top of one another can push anyone to the brink. Rob Brandagee and Ava DeMarco, the owners of Little Earth, have a set of rules set up to keep from killing one another. "We go out and have date nights, where we aren't allowed to talk about the business at all," DeMarco says. "That's great most of the time, but sometimes we're just eating and we don't really have much to say to each other. If we can't talk about the business, and that's what's on your mind most of the time anyway, we don't have much to talk about."

"The really important thing is to spend time away from one another," says Brandagee. For instance, they both make a concerted effort to participate in team sports or athletic activities that don't involve one another. "If you don't do that, you have nothing new to bring to your relationship. You're boring. You're the same two people, spending all your time together every day. I'd go nuts."

Still, it's hard to avoid one another around the house, which can work both ways. "We have this continuous conversation going, so ideas tend to mature faster," says Brandagee. "It's not like we have to schedule time to sit down with one another. When you're sitting down at dinner each night, you're usually talking about it."

"But that's the bad part of it all too," DeMarco adds. "If I go home and I've had a bad day because I've designed something that doesn't work or the printer missed a deadline because I screwed up, I can't go home and complain about how hard work was that day because he's mad at me about it."

HOW PARTNERSHIPS CAN GO AWRY

The one good thing about working with your spouse is that, presumably, you know them as well as any one person can know another. So there probably won't be too many surprises once the business kicks into gear. Friends, however, may surprise you sometimes. When Dave Kapell ended up with a good friend as a partner, it was sort of by default. His friend approached him just as Magnetic Poetry was taking off, and Kapell was putting in 80-hour weeks but barely keeping up. "He suggested hiring him to manage the business in return for a share of the profits so that I could just concentrate on doing the creative work," Kapell recalls. "I figured he was a nice guy, a smart guy, and that that would be enough. But within the first week, I knew it had been a big mistake. I normally don't have trouble turning over the reins to someone, but I knew how to run the business and I could just see him about to make these huge mistakes. He thought I was micromanaging him. Finally, it got so bad that he had to go. He became one of our vendors, doing fulfillment on the orders we get over one of our 800 numbers, but he's struggled since and he feels terribly slighted by the whole thing.

"Partnering up with someone is at least as serious as getting married," continues Kapell, "probably more so since you spend more of your waking hours with your business partner than with your spouse. But most people don't think about it that way. You better be damn well sure you want to marry this person who's going to be your partner. You have to be certain of your love. Don't get into business with someone because you have a crush on them." This may sound sort of funny as you read this on the page, but when Kapell talks about it, his voice drips with exhaustion, exasperation, and regret.

Even if you're certain you've picked the right friend to go into business with, at least consider the possibility that the worst could happen. Is it worth it? "You never start a business with a friend unless you're willing to see that relationship go," says Gary Alpert of Wet Feet Press, who started the company with a close friend from Stanford Business School. "We discussed that a lot in the very beginning, and you try to talk yourself out of the fact that it could happen to you, but the truth is, it could happen to anyone. We decided we were willing to take on that risk."

Amicable break-ups happen as well, often when the partners can at least come to some agreement that one of them isn't willing to put the time in that's necessary to start a real company. "There were three of us at first," notes CDNow's Jason Olim. "We all still had other jobs at that point, and we wrote up a business plan and I started putting together the computer code. Within a couple weeks, they said 'You know what? We'd have to quit our jobs to do this.' And I said, 'You know what, yeah, you would.' And they pretty much stopped working with [CDNow] right after that."

Since it was not yet clear how successful Olim was going to be, his partners didn't have any qualms about cutting loose. Unfortunately, things don't always work out that neatly, and you may find yourself needing to give your deadweight a gentle shove in the direction of the door. "We had one friend who wanted to invest but not quit his day job," notes Scott Samet of Taste of Nature. "He was supposed to be helping with accounting and some other things, but he got very busy with his other job. There was all this shit that just wasn't getting done. We understood, but he just couldn't handle both and he didn't realize it." Adds Samet's partner, Doug Chu: "He didn't want out, but he was excess baggage, so we gave him a price for his share that he was happy with, and we're still friendly."

GOING SOLO

No matter what kind of partner you have, there are going to be trade-offs: you'll always have someone to turn to, but you'll always have someone to fight with as well.

Marcia Kilgore of Bliss was more concerned about the latter when she first got started, for, like Dave Kapell, she had been burned by a partner before. When Kilgore first started giving facials out of her apartment, she and a partner were also busy distributing imported beauty supplies. The whole thing came unraveled when the guy brought his girlfriend into the business and then froze Kilgore out. Now he's suing her, claiming that she quit when she was contractually obligated to continue to help him, and he wants damages to make up for the business he says he's lost. Kilgore would just as soon not take the risk of ending up partnered with someone else who's litigious, so Bliss remains a solo venture.

If you're extremely confident and steadfast in your vision of what you want your company to be, working with a partner may cause too much tension. "I knew myself well enough to know that it clearly had to be done my way," says Vendemmia's Todd Alexander. "I wasn't worried about the logistics and the manpower, because you can hire people to stock your warehouse and drive your truck and sell your wine. I had my vision, and once I was focused on it and believed it would work, I don't think it would have helped to have a partner telling me otherwise."

While it's true that Jeffrey Hyman needed a partner to help him program Career Central's computers, and Kevin Donlin's home-based résumé business probably works better with one boss, there's a large middle ground. Marcia Kilgore could probably use an equal to help take the load off, given how successful her business has become. Others could probably be run by only one person. In other words, it's not the type of business that determines whether you need a partner—it's your frame of mind and style of work that matter. Just don't be too stubborn about it. It's never too late to bring in a partner as an equal. And you're not admitting failure if you need to cut a partner—or even yourself—loose from a business relationship that's so bad that it could kill the enterprise.

CHAPTER 5

MAKING MONEY GROW ON TREES

Finding the Cash to Feed Your Business

So who's going to pay for it all?

If you don't have a million-dollar trust fund at your disposal, fear not. Michael Dell didn't have two cents to rub together when he started assembling computers in his dorm room. The hardest part about getting money isn't necessarily finding someone who will lend you some. Rather, it's guessing how much you'll actually need to get your business up and running. One of the biggest reasons great ideas don't become great businesses is because their founders ran out of money. You probably already know this, so you don't need another lecture on undercapitalization. But how can you possibly know how much cash you need to keep your business afloat until it generates its own?

WRITE A BUSINESS PLAN, EVEN IF NO ONE ELSE WILL SEE IT

Normally, the business plan is the tome you prepare for banks or venture capitalists to convince them that you have some idea of what you're doing (even though nobody, no matter what their age, ever quite does). So what does a business plan look like, and what can it do for you? There are whole books out there that focus solely on how to write a business plan, so I won't bore you with samples and outlines here (check out the Resource Section for a list of some of the better guides). Essentially, though, it's just a fairly detailed explanation of what you plan to do (that's your great idea); why you think it will work given your industry, the competition, and customer demand (remember that market research you did?); and what kind of money you think it will take to put yourself in a position to earn whatever it is you think you can ultimately earn (that's the hard part, so we'll tackle it in the first part of this chapter before we discuss where all this money will come from).

People who use their own cash, borrow from generous friends and relatives, or rack up credit card debt often skip the business plan, since they don't need to talk any strangers into investing in their start-up. But this can be a huge mistake, especially since these plans aren't all that difficult to produce. You probably have about 80 percent of the crucial issues outlined in your head already. Committing them to paper will crystallize them further and help you spot the weak points in your logic. "If you can't articulate it on paper, then your objectives are probably not clear. Chances are, then, that you're not going to reach your goals," says Kevin Donlin of Guaranteed Resumes. Sure, your plan is bound to be only a rough draft, but that's all right. "It's a work in progress," Donlin adds, "but you have to start somewhere."

So, about those financial projections. Don't worry if you sit down with a pad of paper and a calculator and feel totally clueless. Amy Nye Wolf was coming off a couple years at Goldman Sachs, which trains some of the best young financial minds in America, when she started Altitunes, and even she felt somewhat adrift. "At Goldman, they teach you to do what's known as comps, which is using information from publicly held companies in an industry to establish benchmarked projections for another company that does or could compete in that same industry," she says. "But the joke in our group was that you could add up the weights of the people on our study team, divide by 6, and add 42 and still come close to the right answer."

Although it was all so seemingly random, Wolf still gave it her best shot when she started Altitunes. "Anything sounds feasible when you've never done it before," she explains, noting the unfailing optimism with which everyone should approach this sort of thing. "I tried to guess how many CDs I could sell each hour. The airport people gave me data about the number of passengers who got on a plane each hour, so I figured out what percentage of those needed to stop and buy something for my business to work. They also gave me the dollars spent per enplaned passenger for each of the stores already there, which helped a lot too. The sunglasses store was getting about 10 cents per passenger, while the newsstand got about $1.20. I figured I'd be in the middle somewhere. Not as many people want a CD as a newspaper, but I figured maybe I'd sell more units than the sunglasses people did. I figured on 15 cents per passenger, and that turned out to be pretty accurate."

As Wolf's example demonstrates, you don't necessarily need training from Goldman Sachs to figure this stuff out. Elizabeth Burke and Abby Messitte both studied art as undergraduates, yet their financial projections for their gallery turned out to be pretty close to reality. "Unfortunately, a lot of people in the business weren't willing to share their budget numbers with us or tell us how much anything had cost them," Burke says. While they did the right thing by asking people in their industry for help, the gallery world is as brutally competitive as they come, so there was no guarantee that they were going to get any assistance. So they just pressed on and made the best guesses they could about what the numbers would look like. "We had to figure rent, lighting, building walls, putting on the shows, insurance, our minimal salaries, and budget for whatever surprises might come up. We came up with $60,000 as our very bare-bones projections for the first year, and we were actually quite close to that."

LET YOUR BUSINESS FEED ITSELF

Once you have a rough idea of what kind of money you think you'll need, it's time to go out and get it. There are three basic ways this can happen, though each has a number of variations within it. The first one is to simply let the business feed itself, which assumes that you can start it for nothing and that the money it brings in will be enough to fuel your growth. The second is to rely on your own financial resources: savings, a second job, credit cards, or whatever else you have at your own personal disposal. Finally, you can bring others into the game: friends, family, banks, venture capitalists—the list of people who would love to make money off your hard work is practically endless.

As you can see, I've listed these three categories in rough order of desirability. Obviously, the less you have to spend, the better, which is why it's nice if the business essentially pays for itself. If that's not possible, though, you're better off putting your own money up if you can rather than paying interest to someone else or giving them a percentage of ownership in your company in return for their cash.

So what kinds of businesses launch themselves? A lot of them, actually, can do just fine for a year or two without any cash infusion other than the sales that they generate. The key is sweat equity, and all that's based on is your own personal stamina—the ability to repeatedly endure all-nighters to get your business started. It helps if you're your own best asset and your only product too, as Alex Kramer and Kevin Donlin are. Because they're in service businesses, where their only products are the things they do for people, they don't need to invest much in factories or other employees.

Still, running a service business isn't your only option if you're practically penniless. Before the Gardner brothers went online with their personal finance musings, they had started a print newsletter. "We figured if we could get 1,000 subscriptions at $48 each, that would work out great," Tom Gardner recalls. While about 3 percent of the people they pitched ended up subscribing—a fantastic ratio for a start-up publication—that added up to only about 35 people. "We kept thinking it had been delayed in the mail, because we figured that we had put together something so great that people who didn't know us in North Dakota would want to spend money for something like this."

They never landed 1,000 subscriptions, but it didn't matter. Soon after they sent out those solicitations, the brothers caught the online bug and eventually set up their own folder on America Online—which anyone can do. Right away, lots of people started noticing them, since AOL members didn't have to pay anything to access the Motley Fool site specifically. "One day we got a call from AOL, and they said 'Hey, you guys have a following. How about coming to have lunch with us.' It was very convenient that their headquarters in Vienna, Virginia, were just 25 minutes from our house," David recalls. "We ended up signing a deal with them where they gave us 8 percent of usage, which meant that if someone was paying $10 an hour to access AOL and spent an hour in Motley Fool, AOL would give us 80 cents."

As the site grew even more popular, Motley Fool's cut more than doubled. To this day, they've never had to borrow a dime from anyone to keep the business up and running, even though they now have over 100 employees on the payroll. Collegiate Sales and Marketing and Magnetic Poetry have also never been forced into debt or drawn much on their owners' bank accounts, because the cash they've generated has been enough to pay overhead, buy supplies, and hire additional employees.

A more creative but somewhat risky way to keep your business up and running without a big financial infusion is to master what's known as the float. Jason Olim of CDNow discovered this method before he even knew what it was called, but he ended up using it to great advantage. "I was keeping track of our finances using Quicken," he says, "and I had called up a friend of mine who was in business school to ask him something. Quicken said that we owed just $30,000 to the wholesaler that supplied us with CDs, but the bank said we had more than $50,000 on hand. How could that be? He explained that when people charge CDs on their credit cards, we get the money in three days, but we don't have to pay our suppliers until several weeks after that. That time in between, he said, was the float." In other words, the extra $20,000 would float in CDNow's bank account for a few weeks until it was time to pay the suppliers.

So could a company spend any of that $20,000 and still feel safe? Well, it all depends on how fast you're growing—the faster it's happening, the better this strategy will work. The trick is to figure out if you have enough money from next month's sales to pay the bill that's coming due next month for the stuff that you sold and shipped last month. "We were growing 10, 20, 30 percent a month the first year, so we were able to run the whole thing off the float for a while," Olim says.

HOW YOU CAN FEED YOUR BUSINESS

Not everyone experiences exponential sales growth like that, of course, so let's return to the assumption that the business won't simply pay for itself. The next most attractive option is generally to try to fund it with money you've come up with on your own. If you've already been making money for several years in another job, you may have enough cash saved up to do what you need to do. "Our budget was $70,000 because that's all we had," explains Tom Baron of Mad Mex. "I had a house so I took out a home equity loan. I had money from the settlement of a lawsuit from a motorcycle accident I had been in with someone who had cut me off on the road. Our general manager put in money, and so did Juno." Sure, they could have used some more cash, but they made a decision to spend only what they had at first.

Cash in Your Life Savings

Marcia Kilgore didn't even need to stretch when she first started giving facials. She ran the business out of her apartment for one year, and the money she earned paid for suppliers, rent, and then some. When it came time to move the business out of her house, she didn't need much cash to take it to the next level. "When I had started working as a personal trainer, I was 20," she says, "so I didn't have any overhead because I worked out with people at their homes or at their gyms, plus I didn't really need fabulous shoes or a great wardrobe. As a result of all that, I had put some money away, and it only took about $7,000 to buy the things I needed to move the business out of my apartment. I paid $650 a month for a small office, had a small table, a stereo, and a screened-off changing area. It was no big deal." By continuing to keep her overhead costs low, Kilgore was able to save enough to finance later moves to bigger digs.

Take the Money and Run

You've probably read a fair bit in the past few years about all the people getting fired from jobs in companies both large and small. The irony in those sorts of situations—which human resources staffers and outplacement counselors love to mention—is that getting canned could end up being one of the best things that's ever happened to you. And for some people (especially those who walk away with a lot of money from their severance packages), this actually ends up being true, since they can use that cash as seed capital for starting their own company.

Take Little Earth, for instance. When Rob Brandagee first dreamed up the idea of making bags and other accessories out of recycled goods, his girlfriend, Ava, was a partner in a small graphic design firm in Pittsburgh. "I had worked for various companies in the field at the beginning of my career, and then two people recruited me out of a big firm to join their firm," she recalls. She eventually became a full financial partner in the business. With the money she made as a designer, she was able to invest about $10,000 in Little Earth and also help Rob at night with the work.

"We grew the design firm into a $3 million company," DeMarco continues, "doing annual reports for corporations, recruiting brochures, and things like that. When Rob started Little Earth, I cut back from probably 70 hours a week to 55. Clients would ask me about Little Earth all the time, and it infuriated my partners because they didn't think I was working hard enough. The straw that broke the camel's back there was when my grandmother got sick and I missed a deadline when I went to see her. They just assumed I had missed the deadline because I was doing too much work for Little Earth. So one Friday they called me in and told me that they were firing me. They just bought out my shares in the partnership and let me go." Though DeMarco was devastated, it didn't take her long to figure out where to put the money they had given her in return for her going away.

Another advantage of starting a business with your significant other is that the two of you can do exactly what Brandagee and DeMarco were doing early on, using one person's disposable income to fund a business that belongs to both of you. Think about it this way: if you believe that your spouse and his or her business is a good investment, then it's really no different than putting that money in mutual funds or in your company's 401(k) plan. "You put small amounts in over time, so it may not end up seeming like $50,000, which is what it ended up being in our case," says Andy Spade, who was a copywriter for an ad agency in New York City while his wife, Kate, was starting their handbag company. "We hadn't set a certain amount aside. It was a few thousand to get the fabric, then a few more to go to market. That's a much better way to think about it."

If you don't have a romantic partner who wants to become your business partner, you can still make this cohabitation strategy work. When Gary Alpert and Steve Pollock graduated from Stanford Business School, neither of them had found permanent jobs, since they had intended all along to start a company together. Though Wet Feet Press didn't cost much to start, they still had to eat, so they did consulting projects while simultaneously getting the business started.

Moonlighting

While it's clearly preferable to have everyone who's in on your start-up going at it full-time, that may not be possible if money is tight. So there's no shame in doing a little bit of moonlighting too, if that's what it takes to keep your business up and running. For instance, Elizabeth Burke and Abby Messitte take time off from their gallery to work a few days each week at part-time jobs. "It really sucks, but we can do it because there are two of us," Burke says. "But it's really hard. After having already worked full-time for somebody else for eight years, it's really humbling to still have to do it two days a week when I own my own business. After taking so much initiative five days a week, it's not fun to have to file somebody's shit or go get them lunch." Of course, that's much better than having to do that stuff full-time. And both women know that eventually, if they put the time in at Clementine, they won't have to work for anyone else at all.

In the meantime, theirs is not a bad way to ease in to running your own business if it's not the kind of thing that can simply take off right away. For instance, Kevin Donlin didn't have the cash to do the marketing to attract enough clients to make Guaranteed Resumes a full-time gig right off the bat. "I worked 20 hours a week for a local marketing firm," he explains. "It was flex-time, which meant that I could do the work whenever I wanted. But the paycheck was still regular. I probably could have made the résumé service work on a full-time basis if I had fewer expenses, but my wife and I had our first baby on the way and we have house payments to make, so I didn't want to completely quit that marketing job." After fifteen months, he built the business to the point where he could run it full-time.

GETTING OTHERS TO FEED YOUR BUSINESS

What if you don't have any savings or a big severance check from the assholes who pushed you out of your last job? In that case, it might be time to think about hitting up your family. At first glance, this doesn't seem like the most attractive option. After all, they've probably supported you while you were growing up and maybe through college as well. Perhaps they let you live at home while you were at an age when many of your peers were living on their own. At this point, they probably deserve to be done with the financial burdens that come from having kids around. Plus, who wants to ask for a handout anyway?

Dear Mom and Dad

If you swallow your pride for a minute, however, you may see the wisdom in all this. "If you think about all the options, borrowing from your parents makes the most sense. That's where the rates are best," says Dave Hirschkop of Dave's Gourmet. Family members may be willing to give you an interest-free loan, but even if they don't, they're probably not likely to charge usurious rates. Plus, as Hirschkop notes, the payment plan is generally a little more flexible. "There may be a point where you can't make the month's payment, but the rules you live by in this sort of situation are a little different. If you miss one, you probably won't be out in the street."

Missing the rent payment on your office won't be a problem, however, if you convince your parents to literally take you under their wings. "I moved back into their house," says Jason Olim, founder of CDNow, who soon had his brother back at home working on it as well. "I would work from 10 A.M. to 2 A.M. and Matt would work from 4 P.M. to 8 A.M. I lost a girlfriend over it, but it didn't take a lot of money. The fact that our folks really believed in us, that they were literally there every step of the way, really fed us too." Olim's parents invested some money as well, but it was the roof over their sons' heads that was the biggest contribution to getting CDNow off the ground.

There is one danger here. Remember those "You can be anything you want to be" speeches you used to get from your family when you were a kid? Their faith in you is still probably so blind that they can't see through the holes in your business plan to the bankruptcy on the other side. Harry Gottlieb, who started Jellyvision, a CD-ROM and Internet content developer that conceived of the "You Don't Know Jack" series of games, first hit up his father for funds for an educational film he wanted to make. "He wouldn't give it to me at first," Gottlieb recalls. "He said that if I couldn't find someone who didn't love me who was willing to put up the money, then it probably wasn't worth doing. Once

I did that, my father was willing to invest." That's probably a pretty smart strategy.

Credit Card Bingo

If your family doesn't have any money to loan you (or they've taken a look at your business plan and decided that you're nuts), there are other people you can turn to. For many young entrepreneurs, the first instinct is to hit up those generous folks at the credit card companies. As you may have noticed in your mailbox recently, the world of plastic has changed dramatically in the last ten years. Practically every bank, from the smallest community banks to the biggest conglomerates, have slapped their names on Visas and MasterCards in the past decade. Meanwhile, dozens of companies have sprouted up that do nothing but issue credit cards.

They all have to get their business somewhere, so that's why you've seen so many solicitations in your mailbox. The trick to exploiting this system is taking advantage of what's known in credit card land as the teaser rate. Companies will offer you, say, an 8 percent annual interest rate on the balance you carry from month to month in return for transferring your balance from the card you already have to the one that they want you to sign up for. The catch is, the teaser usually expires within three to twelve months, and then the interest rate doubles. The trick? Just stay one step ahead of the game by transferring your balance to a new card every time the teaser expires.

Think the credit card companies won't want to take you on if you've shown a history of carrying big balances? It's not so. Remember, the more you owe at the time you transfer your debt to their card, the more interest you'll pay on that balance and the more money they'll make. The only thing they care about when you apply is if you've sent in the minimum payment on time for other cards that you've held in the past. This will show up on the credit check that all credit card companies run on you before they solicit your business.

All told, this is not such a bad way to start a company, given how many places take credit cards these days. "Once I saw we had some money coming in and could actually pay the monthly payments, out came the credit cards," says Tom Baron, cofounder of Mad Mex restaurant in Pittsburgh. "I applied for cards. My wife applied for cards. And we used them to pay for everything, from lumber and paint to restaurant equipment and alcohol." At Little Earth, Rob Brandagee and Ava DeMarco pulled a similar scheme, racking up $25,000 in debt by maxing out the credit limits on six or seven cards, and paid for much of their office and factory equipment. "You just operate on total faith that you will be able to pay it all back," Brandagee says.

You can also use a lot of these cards to get cash advances, though the limit on what you can take out is generally much smaller than the limit on the amount of things you can actually buy on the card. The interest rate on cash advances may also be higher, depending on the card you choose. Check the fine print carefully before you fill your wallet with these things.

Take It to the Bank

If you're not at the point where you can make regular monthly payments, or you simply can't use credit cards to pay for the things you need to get your business off the ground, you're going to have to seek help elsewhere. And you may be surprised to learn that it's still quite possible to get your seed capital the old-fashioned way: by borrowing money from a bank. With all the talk these days about venture capital and angel investors and such (don't worry, we'll get there), many entrepreneurs have forgotten that there are still plenty of lending institutions out there that are happy to take a chance on young entrepreneurs under the right conditions.

First of all, they need to understand what you're doing. A loan officer at a community bank, for instance, may not understand your software, though if you're in northern California, there's a better chance that they might. Similarly, if you're on the cutting edge of any industry, you're likely to be met with quizzical glances. For instance, most loan officers have probably seen business plans for health clubs before, but not the sort that Chris and Pam Schmick were planning to build at Upper Limits. "Banks don't know anything about rock climbing," Pam says.

In fact, most people in the Midwest have never experienced the sport of rock climbing; much of that area of the country is flat, so there are very few rocks for people to scale. To overcome this, they presented every loan officer they met with an inch-and-a-half-thick business plan with pictures and statistics to explain the whole concept. "I didn't get the impression that they thought we were stupid kids, though I think they were really surprised that we had such a good proposal. Some people don't even have a proposal when they first come in." Eventually a local bank agreed to give them a loan, though Chris's grandmother had to agree to back them up if anything went awry. This is another important tip, as it's another way your family can help you out without spending a dime up front. Of course they need to be willing to gather a bunch of dimes if your business fails and you need a bailout.

As you'll recall, before John Chuang's business became a temp agency lending out Macintosh computer specialists, it was a storefront renting out time on computers that the company used to do typesetting for other local businesses in Cambridge, Massachusetts. Before they could even do that, though, they needed cash to buy the equipment in the first place. So they went to the local community bank in Cambridge.

"The laser printer cost $5,000 at the time, and we didn't have $5,000," Chuang recalls. "So we wrote this business plan about what sort of business we were running and brought it to the bank. And they said nope, we're not going to give you a loan. They didn't really care about our business. They're not venture capitalists. They just cared about how we were going to pay them back." While Chuang exaggerates slightly here, his point is a good one. Sure, the banks need to buy in to your business vision, but if you can't prove to them that the business will generate the cash to pay them back, or if you don't have personal assets to hock in the event that it doesn't, then the loan officer will probably show you the door.

"So we rewrote the entire business plan," Chuang says. "But we didn't describe what we were going to do with their money once they gave it to us. We described how we were going to pay them back, where the cash flow would come from, and how we would sell the store if things didn't work out. A month went by, and they finally gave us the money once all of our parents agreed to cosign the loan."

Seems like a lot of hassle for a measly five grand? Couldn't they have just charged it on one of those credit cards that show up in every freshman's mailbox? "The beauty of the whole thing is that once they gave us that first five grand, we were able to build a relationship with our bankers at the same time that our business was blooming," Chuang says. When their storefront morphed into MacTemps, Chuang was able to wrangle more money out of the bank's loan officer. "We told him that the reason why the bank wanted to lend us cash was that we had receivables, customers who owned us money for our services. And those receivables were great collateral for the loan, because they weren't just with one company [who could blow the whole deal if they refused to pay up]. They were with lots of little companies. It was much less risky than lending money to a store with inventory, because you never know if the inventory will actually sell.

"So we paid back the ten thousand, but then we would run out of cash, and each time we did, we went back to the bank and explained why we needed more money, and our credit limit went from five thousand to 10 to 30 to 60 to 140 to 320 to 720 to 1.2 million, where we outgrew their legal limit. By the time we left, we were the bank's largest commercial credit customer. We built the whole company through debt, and it was all because we had gone through the pain early on of establishing a relationship with the local bank.

"The other nice thing about it was that it was a small community bank, so we were dealing with the senior vice president of lending. Now if we as a group of kids had gone to a bigger bank, they would have put us with the loan officer with the least experience and the least authority. That person would have just cranked us through their financial ratios and given up on us. It's not the kind of relationship you want.

"I really like the strategy of young entrepreneurs working with a small bank and dealing with people who are higher up there, because the banker does get really involved with your business. The banker is a great source of advice. Ours made us get an accountant, and the accountant reminded us that we should probably be paying taxes. The banker made us get a lawyer and write bylaws." All such details tend to be far from your mind in the frenzy of a start-up, yet big messes can result later on if you haven't dealt with them early on.

VENTURE CAPITALISTS AND ANGEL INVESTORS

Of course, there are other ways you can get that money—and some highly specialized advice along with it—though it comes with costs that are harder to gauge. Venture capitalists (VCs) are a relatively new breed of financiers. Like banks, they lend money to infant businesses. But the way banks get their money back is by asking for regular payments with interest. While the bank has some risk, they usually have some sort of collateral to back themselves up in the event that your business fails. What VCs do to protect themselves is simply take ownership of a percentage of your business. So even if four out of five of their investments fail, the one that doesn't will make up for it because their $1 million investment is often worth many times that a few years down the road. Obviously, it doesn't make sense to give up a fifth of your company unless you're looking for really big bucks and don't have the collateral that a bank would want.

A close cousin of the VCs are a group of people generally known as angel investors. Angels cut similar deals taking a piece of your business in exchange for a cash investment, but there are some important differences between these two groups of investors. Whereas most VCs work in groups, sort of like a small law firm, most angels work alone, though they often bring friends in on deals. So you may not be able to get as much money as quickly from angels as you would from VCs. Generally, angels are more helpful with investments of $50,000 to $500,000, with VCs looking only at deals that are bigger than that. Because they tend to go solo, angels will usually take less time to make up their minds about where they're going to invest their money. And because there are a lot more angels than there are VC firms, you're more likely to find someone with the exact sort of industry expertise that can make them a terrific resource for you and your business.

So how do you find these people? There are plenty of directories, both in print and online, and I've listed some of the best of them in the Resource Section at the end of the book. Angels tend to be a little bit harder to find, since many of them do this sort of thing more as a hobby than anything else. Still, chances are, they are all around you, and you just don't know it. Plenty of them are semiretired, though they're not all old. Lots of them have gotten rich off stock that they picked up working for fast-growing companies that went public in the 1980s, like Microsoft and many of the other technology companies on the West Coast. Others have sold their own upstart start-ups for big bucks and keep their entrepreneurial juices flowing by placing bets on young people who remind them of themselves.

As with any issue that you're facing when you're starting your own company, this is one where the big-mouth method can work wonders. Get on the phone and talk to everyone you can who might know someone who knows someone who does this sort of thing. Having someone introduce you to investors will help, though it's definitely possible to meet these people without any sort of connections.

When Jeffrey Hyman and Lun Yuen started Career Central for

MBAs, they didn't have much of their own money, and they knew that they would need a lot of it to create an enormous database of candidates for companies to hire from. "This wasn't going to be something that we could bootstrap," Hyman says. "If you're going to sign up the number of candidates you need to reach a critical mass, you need a lot of money for sales and marketing. It's like opening a store or something, because we were going to have to go out and convince all these M.B.A.'s to give us their information."

Hyman also believes that putting your idea out to sophisticated investors for review is a pretty good litmus test. "Maybe it's a chicken-shit way to approach something like this, but I felt that if the money didn't come through, then it wasn't a good enough concept. In an efficient market, that's what happens."

So how did they know how much money they would need? "Half of it was out of our ass," Hyman admits. "We knew we needed a database, but we weren't sure what it would look like and how much it would cost to build it. Then, it was the branding that was going to be crucial, getting our name out to schools and using them as our distribution channel to get the software to the alumni so they could e-mail their information to us to put in the database. The economics of what came afterwards was the least of our concerns, since we knew what headhunters charged and figured that even if we were charging one-tenth of what they charged we could still make money. So we set a goal of $700,000 in the first round of financing and told ourselves that if we couldn't get at least $300,000 we'd forget about it."

The temptation here is generally to raise as much money as you possibly can so you don't have to hold another round of fund-raising soon afterwards. However, with each month you stay in business and prove you can get to the next step (for Career Central for MBAs the next step was successfully building the database and getting some schools interested), the more value your business has. Let's say you need to raise $1 million over two years. If you take all that investor money at the beginning and give them a 50 percent stake in your company, when investors value your idea at, say, $500,000, then you're left with the other half, which is worth $250,000. If your business is worth $1 million one year later, you have only half that. But let's say you take only half that $1 million up front, in return for a quarter of your equity instead of the original half, and wait a year to raise the rest. You'll still have $750,000 of equity yourself, which hopefully will continue to grow at a fast clip. Sure, you'll still have to give away some more equity to get the remaining $500,000, but that will be coming out of a much bigger pie, and one that you kept more of for yourself initially. This is known in the trade as avoiding dilution, and it's a strategy that worked well for Career Central. Just be careful not to leave yourself short of cash; if it took three months to raise the first round of money, you'd better start raising the second round three months before you think you'll need it.

Though the brothers of Motley Fool have had the luxury of being able to avoid giving up any equity to outsiders, if they could go back and do it over again, they might actually do things a little differently. "One thing that's useful for young entrepreneurs to do is to give up a percent or two maybe in exchange for free services," says Tom Gardner. "What if you could get everything free for life from Kinko's in return for that small piece of your business?" It's hard to imagine a national chain working that way, but it can't hurt to ask. You may well be able to cut a deal like that with your accountant, lawyer, public relations firm, or consultant.

So once you've figured out how much money you'll need and how quickly you'll need it, you've got to go out and hunt it down. "I didn't know anyone," says Hyman, who notes that even though he had an M.B.A. from Northwestern, it's primarily the West Coast schools and Harvard that bring you into contact with lots of investors. "I started with a couple of angels, not Silicon Valley people but just friends of friends, people that I knew had money," he says. "One basically led to the next one, because even if the people I tracked down weren't interested, they'd usually have a couple of other names of investors who might like the idea more. You'd be surprised at who you can get on the phone if you're persistent enough. I talked to the guy who started 1-800-Flowers because someone had referred me to him, and he came pretty close to putting money in. The guy who started the video game company that did Donkey Kong Country ended up investing, and he got me on the phone with the head of Nintendo, who passed. But at least he talked to me. I also talked to a lot of investment banking partners and consultants who did some angel investing on the side."

One advantage that Hyman and Yuen had was that most of these people had done a fair bit of hiring in the past, and they all remembered what an enormous pain in the ass it had been. So even if they didn't quite understand how all the database technology was going to work, they knew the service that it supported would make life easier for a lot of hiring managers.

Still, it was tough to get the first investor to actually write a check. "They're sort of like vultures, all waiting around to see when someone else is going to dive in," Hyman says. "The polite term for it is soft-circling. Once the first one jumps, then all the dominoes begin to fall. In the meantime, you have to do everything you can to hype it up without lying. You just have to tell them that time is running out, that there's a lot of interest, a lot of demand."

Many others found their investors more or less by accident. Though savings and credit cards helped get the first Mad Mex open in Pittsburgh, once Tom Baron and Juno Yoon saw how successful it was, they were itching to clone it and bring some new restaurant concepts to Pittsburgh as well. One day, Baron recalls, this guy called about how his daughter went to the University of Pittsburgh and how much he'd liked eating at Mad Mex. "He had a real estate partner, and the two of them wanted to invest. We sat down, and two hours later we shook hands on a deal." This sort of thing actually happens more than you might think. If you do a good enough job, some of your customers will be so moved by your talent and energy that they'll end up wanting to invest in you.

When Elizabeth Burke and Abby Messitte were preparing to launch Clementine, they weren't quite sure where to turn for start-up money. Plus, they had to contend with the problematic image of the art world itself. "There's a real sense that it's just a bunch of slackers working in the art community," says Burke. "There's a lot of talk about doing things that never actually get done. Generally, no one takes you seriously until you have already rented gallery space." Which, of course, was impossible, since they hadn't raised enough money to do that.

"At that point, we just started going out and schmoozing, going to as many gallery openings as we could and just talking to everyone about what we were doing," says Burke. Here's the "big mouth" strategy again. The more people who know what you're up to, the more likely you are to find someone who can help you. And it worked for Burke and Messitte. "A friend called one day and invited me to an opening because she said I ought to meet her brother," Messitte recalls. "I was sick, and I didn't want to go, but I did. He told me that he had heard about our gallery and was really interested. I didn't think anything of it, but then he found my number and called. Turns out he and his mother invested a lot of money."

You're probably less likely to run into a venture capitalist at a party than you are to bump into an art patron, so your search for VCs will have to be a bit more structured. Thankfully, they're easier to find than patrons, as most of them are listed in directories or are members of national organizations. The founders of Career Central, which is based in Palo Alto, can barely drive down the street without passing the offices of a VC firm, but at first they decided to keep going right by. "At first we didn't consider venture capitalists, mostly because the ones out where we are tend to invest only in companies that have some sort of proprietary technology," Hyman says.

"While our business was technology enabled, it was basically an execution play. Anybody with some money could replicate what we planned to do relatively easily, and if they did, then it would just be a fight to see who could do it better. Most venture capitalists out here aren't interested in getting involved in something like that, plus they also tend to invest in companies that are at least a little bit past the seed stage, which we weren't. So we thought maybe we'd try them when we were ready for our second round. But it turned out that Softbank Technology Ventures, which is the venture capital arm of a big Japanese company, was interested in investing in the career arena and didn't mind investing seed capital."

As we discussed earlier, venture capitalists are fairly demanding sorts, and it's not just your equity that they want. Most of them want you to bow to them too, which is something that Jason Olim learned the hard way when he was trying to interest them in investing in CDNow. "When I first met with some of them, I could see that they thought that I was this kid who didn't know anything about business," he says. "I didn't put on a suit for them. I didn't understand their lingo or the methodology they used to put a value on the company. They looked at me like a dumb kid who was going to get his ass kicked. I was actually treated pretty badly."

Olim knew he needed some pointers on his presentation techniques, so he met with a former executive from his old company who dabbled in venture investing. "He asked me to give him the pitch I had been giving to the VCs," Olim recalled. "He told me that I needed to focus my spiel and tighten things up a bit. But the most important thing he told me was that I had to learn to kiss his ass. It all goes back to playing up to the ego of the VC. They care whether you're going to respect what they have to say. From the beginning, I had built the business on the premise that of course I was going to learn from everyone around me and run it based on consensus. So as soon as I began working that into my pitch, and saying here's where you, the VC, could come in and give us advice, a lot of people became interested." Olim ultimately kept it simple by dealing with just one firm to coordinate the financing.

While you're busy kissing up, however, don't forget that you have some cards in your own hand. Given the research you've probably already done, you could teach these investor people a few things about the industry you intend to storm through. Venture capitalists and the smart angel investors know this, and they're more than happy to have you in for an hour or two to educate them, even when they have no intention of investing in your company. "We thought money was money," Hyman recalls. After several visits with investors who seemed fascinated and then never called again, he and Yuen realized that they ought to investigate these people beforehand to see if they'd ever be interested in investing in a company like the one they hoped to create.

Since venture capitalists lend money for a living and not as a hobby, they tend to be fairly professional, even if they are a bit sleazy, as the anecdote suggests. It's relatively easy to find other entrepreneurs they've worked with, so you can check up on them to make sure they don't run their investment portfolio as if it were Nazi Germany. When you're working with angels, however, especially inexperienced ones, there's a much better chance of running into someone who has no clue how to behave in a relationship like this. So just make sure you have plenty of conversations with any potential angels before agreeing to take their money. "There was a woman who came in to get her legs waxed who owned a big publishing company," recalls Marcia Kilgore of Bliss. "She and her husband said they didn't know anything about the spa business, but they just wanted to invest. They even had a building nearby where we could have moved.

"But then we started to negotiate, and it became such a nightmare. Suddenly, they wanted to lend me the money I needed to expand at an interest rate that was over the prime rate, rent me their space, and take 25 percent of the business. And what was in it for me? Then, she wanted to consult on everything from the music to the carpet to the name. And I had thought at first that

they didn't know anything about the spa business. Eventually, I couldn't even stand the sound of her voice on my answering machine. The negotiations were totally taking the fun out of it, and this is supposed to be a fun business, with people wearing mud on their faces walking around in robes eating crackers and drinking wine. And it got to the point where I would have rather slit my wrists and jumped off a bridge than work with them. So I got out."
No one should ever get that close to going nuts. If you're getting bad vibes from a potential investor, just give it up and start looking for someone new.

Jeffrey Hyman and Lun Yuen probably could have ended up doing without some of the people who invested in Career Central during their first round of financing. "People don't understand the word *venture,"* says Hyman. "You might as well be going to Vegas if you're going to be investing in start-ups. We had some people who were investing as angels for the first time. They tend to write the smallest checks, the $15,000 or $20,000 people, but they take up the most amount of your time. One guy was running spreadsheets on our projections that I hadn't even done myself."

One smart thing Hyman and Yuen did was keep the terms they set with investors pretty simple. "Everyone got the same deal," Hyman says. "Sometimes people will give better deals to the VCs or to the people who came in on the first round, but we decided not to. One investment banker who invested some of his own money wanted us to sign an agreement that said that if anyone else got better terms than him, we would have to match it and give it to him too. So we just decided not to mess around with it, since the advice we had gotten was to keep it clean. Softbank wanted to make a few adjustments, so we made the same adjustments for everyone." The partners ended up giving up about a third of the company on the first round.

As you can tell from reading so far, every source of financing comes with its own set of risks and rewards, which usually increase in direct proportion with one another. If you're not interested in getting too far into debt, there are plenty of service businesses and others that don't require much start-up capital. But if you need a big hunk of cash, you'll probably have to loosen your reins on the business sooner or later and give up some equity. After all, if you don't find enough money to invest in your growing company, the risks are pretty high as well. Kate Spade, who gave equity to two partners in return for some cash and sweat equity, puts it this way: "The question is, do you want 100 percent of nothing or some smaller percent of something?"

Put in those terms, the choice seems rather obvious.

CHAPTER 6

GUERRILLA MARKETING

How to Stand Out When No One's Paying Attention

If nobody knows your business exists, it doesn't really matter how good your idea is. This is something that you should be thinking about from day one.

YOU WANT TO BE WHERE EVERYBODY KNOWS YOUR NAME

Most traditional marketing is really expensive. Fortunately, however, you can do a lot of other things to spread the word about your business, and most of them cost a lot less than advertisements. First of all, you'll need a name. It's worth spending a lot of time thinking about this, because a good one can really set your business apart. Think about how often you'll be dropping your company's name into conversation once you actually pick it. One hundred times a day? One thousand? What about the number of times customers or potential customers will come into contact with it? Thousands? Tens of thousands? It better make a damn good impression. (Also, once it does, you can be sure someone will try to steal it if you don't have it trademarked, so make sure to talk to a lawyer about this.)

An outrageous impression helps too. This was the tack that David and Tom Gardner took when they named their online personal finance site the Motley Fool. "We knew what we wanted to do," David recalls, noting that most personal finance guides at the time were dry, boring, and lacked any sort of edge or attitude. "We just didn't have a name for it. And then we thought of the fool. It's actually a great position to come from, because there's no pretension whatsoever about it. I had read Shakespeare's plays in high school and college, and the fool was always a great character—funny, smart, unusual, distinctive. If we screwed up, well, we were fools anyway and we tried our best. But if we succeeded, well, then that would be a very interesting position. We could tell people to just make of us what they would—we're fools, and meanwhile all the other people out there trying to tell you how to manage your money are wearing pin-stripe suits and trying to look impressive. But they're not succeeding at helping you beat the market. So what are you left with?"

What they were left with was not so much the distinctive image of two brothers in clown suits and Dr. Seuss hats. Instead, the notion of the fool came across as a sly marketing ploy. What it said was that this company's approach to investing would be radically different, and probably a whole lot of fun too. It made the Gardner brothers out to be people just like their customers, instead of all-knowing gurus. What could it hurt for someone to at least check it out on America Online? And once they did, what would keep them from jumping in the discussion areas and offering up their point of view, whatever expertise they could toss in? Nothing, it turns out. Today, the best thing about the Motley Fool is that so many different people do just that, and now the Fool stands for the little guy slugging it out against the Wall Street big guys trying to create a stock portfolio that will beat those so-called pros.

The subtlety of the Fool works quite well, but it's difficult to pull that sort of thing off. So it's fine if you want to take an easier route and have your business's name create a sharp mental image in the minds of your potential customers. "In the first big space I had, the business was called 'Let's Face It,' " says Marcia Kilgore. "But I decided that was a little too sarcastic, because when you're getting a skin treatment, you're not supposed to be facing anything. You're supposed to be forgetting it all for a while. I didn't want anything French, because that would be too poofy. That's not what we are—we're happening people having a good time here. So I just thought about how you would describe the best feeling you could possibly have—happiness, elation. Then it just came to me: Bliss. It's catchy, and we can have a mail order catalog of beauty supplies called Bliss Out and a press kit that says 'Pu-Bliss-Ity' on it. I was lucky that no one else had thought of it before me."

When Robert Stephens set out to create a computer repair service in Minneapolis that would be worlds apart from anything that had come before it, he knew that even the name would have to be truly different. "The first thing I did was to see what the competition called themselves," he recalls. "The same two names were in front of every business in this town—Northern Lights and Twin Cities. Northern Lights Computer Repair, Twin Cities Molding and Dye, and on and on. Then there were the Technodynes and the Cybersystems. In terms of corporate identity, those prefixes are so overused. They've been totally deadened. The meaning is gone."

While the word *geek* isn't exactly underutilized either, no one had ever thought to name their business with the term. "The name of the company needed to do two things," Stephens explained. "It needed to explain that we were a group, even though I was the only member at the time. And it needed to emphasize that we were technical people. So what's a good word for that? *Rocket scientists? Engineers? Nerd* was kind of funny, but *geek* had a great phonetic ring to it. Then it needed an action word to get at the fact that we were a group of people performing a function. After a while, I came up with this idea of a bomb squad. How many people can say they work for a bomb squad?"

So Robert Stephens became the Geek Squad, and while the name doesn't explain exactly what his business does, it conveys enough of a promise of something really interesting that it ends up working quite well. It's all right to be literal too, as long as you don't end up sounding like all those Northern Lights companies. When Kevin Donlin set out to name his résumé consulting business, he looked in the Yellow Pages and laughed at all the companies that had tagged themselves with names like AAA Resumes to be the first enterprise listed alphabetically under "Resumes" in the directory. "There was no niche evident anywhere," he recalls. "No one had made any effort to distinguish themselves other than to be listed first. Now people tell me that they looked at 20 different firms in the phone book and on the Internet, but they called me because my name, 'Guaranteed Resumes,' stuck out. It really is one of my strongest marketing weapons."

If you're not like Donlin and have a product to sell instead of a service, assigning a great name to your most prominent product can give a fledgling business a boost too. "We chose the name 'Dave's Insanity Sauce,' " says Dave Hirschkop, founder of Dave's Gourmet. "The name of the product matches the product, which is the hottest of the hot sauces. You've got to be crazy, just insane, to use it. The label looks that way. The way we conduct ourselves at trade shows backs it up. We even started answering the phone in a way that would make people think we were nuts." In a sea of thousands of hot sauces, that's not a bad way to make yours stand out. And while naming a company after yourself usually reeks of pretension, in the food business it sends a nice message—that there's some guy named Dave somewhere cutting up habaneros so that you can experience the heat yourself.

THE PROFIT IN PANACHE

As Dave Hirschkop suggests, you can't pick a really cool name unless you're willing to back it up with other things that are cool. Sure, your product has to blow people away, and you need to make sure you've raised enough money and all that, but it also helps to have a good sense of style. This isn't as important if you're doing something that no one else has ever done before, like Magnetic Poetry or Career Central for MBAs. But doing things with some flair is crucial if you're entering a business that's already filled with lots of other competitors.

Few people in the world run a business with more flair than

Robert Stephens of the Geek Squad. That may seem strange, given the business that he's in. Sure, being an entrepreneur in any technology-related business is fairly glamorous these days, but very few of those companies can safely be called stylish. My first exposure to Stephens's style was not when he appeared in the *Wall Street Journal*'s "Front Lines" column in 1996 but back in the mid-1980s, when we both hung out at a Chicago juice bar/dance club called Medusa's. Stephens drove around in an old car with a Batman logo painted on the side. He also wore a logo-bedecked trench coat as a cape, just drawing attention to himself by doing his own thing long before the Batman revival took place. "Everyone knew who I was. Skinheads, rich kids, all of them," he says. "I learned a lot back then about how the public perceives something odd.

"That gets into the visual element of my thinking," he says, explaining how anal he was when it came time to design the Geek Squad logo. "In the process of designing it, I spent a lot of time looking at old copies of *Life* magazine from the 1950s," he continues. "There are certain symbols that just haven't changed at all in decades. Texaco. Marlboro. Pampers. Tide. Certain things have a timeless design. I want my company to be around for 50 years, so it's important to pick something that can last that long. It's one of those romantic delusions of grandeur, that if I act like a 50-year-old company maybe I'll actually get there."

Was it really worth Stephens's while to spend so much time poring over ideas for a logo? Well, remember what a competitive industry he was entering, and remember how often people were going to see his logo. For instance, every time someone passes out a business card (and if they're smart, they give them to every single person they meet), they'll make some sort of impression. Stephens figured this out early on. "Ultimately, I picked something that looked kind of like the STP logo," he says. "I had business cards cut in that same oval shape, with two colors and printing on both sides. If someone hands over an ordinary card, no offense, but most people are like, *whoosh,* right into the garbage. I didn't want to hand over my card and not have it be a memory of the Geek Squad experience, so I knew that I had to design something that looked really good."

Of course, the image of that card really did have to be backed up by the experience of having the Geek Squad rescue your hard drive, or else it would all just be a figment of Stephens's overactive imagination. "It all flowed from the original ideas about design," he says. "Eventually, I saw a fleet of cars and people looking like secret agents with badges." He started with the cars. His had just broken down, so he figured that when he got a new one, it should serve as his advertising. He found a Simca—an old French model from the 1950s, a gorgeous mound of curves rarely seen on this side of the ocean—painted it sea green, and slapped the Geek Squad logo on the side.

Once there were employees helping Stephens make service calls, they needed vehicles too. Rather than having them drive their own cars and then reimburse them for the mileage, he collected a sleek fleet of antique cars and old ice cream trucks, repainted them with his logo, and sent them back on the road. Behind the wheel were his employees, dressed in black suits, white button-down, short-sleeve dress shirts, black clip-on ties, and badges.

What was he thinking exactly? "Everything's been done, but

not everything has been combined," he explains. "I'm borrowing everything, from James Bond with his great old cars to imagery from Dragnet and the Blues Brothers. The whole world's a hybrid now, and Geek Squad is Ghostbusters meets Swingers."

Minneapolis had never seen anything quite like it, and soon Stephens and his gang of repairmen were urban folk heroes. They didn't let it get to their heads, though. "If it's just image, then it's not legitimate," he warns. "I always tell my employees, don't ever look at the drivers next to you and smile when you're stopped at a light driving a Geekmobile. If they honk and wave, be nonchalant and acknowledge it. But don't ever look like you're trying to attract attention, because if you do, people don't think it's cool. I want people to really think to themselves: 'Hey, do these people know that they're wearing clip-on ties and driving around in these weird cars that say "Geek" on the license plate?' "

The beauty of all this was that once people got over their surprise, they remembered that there was a business behind it all, and Stephens was flooded with calls. The cost of the Geekmobiles, which was much less than buying plain white vans like most repair companies, was minuscule when you consider the attention it drew. "Honestly, it was all about money," Stephens says. "I didn't have any. I still don't have enough to purchase quarter-page ads in the big newspaper here. I started with $200 and my bike in the middle of winter. It took me three months to get that first car."

TALK IS CHEAP

If you're creative enough to come up with a marketing scheme like the Geek Squad's, people will talk about you plenty. Still, it doesn't hurt to talk about your business yourself. While most people don't like talking a lot about themselves (or hearing someone else talk a lot about themselves), when you're talking about your business, it's a little bit different. You're talking about your job, which is perfectly polite cocktail party conversation. You just happen to have created your own job, which, by the way, will be a lot more interesting to most people you meet than if you worked for a law firm or something.

Guaranteed Resumes's Kevin Donlin takes a more formal approach. "I spam my friends every few months with promotional announcements," he says. "I wouldn't do it with people I didn't know, but my friends don't mind. I just say, 'Hey, you know I'm still writing résumés for a living and here's an update on my new Web site or something like that.'" So don't worry about sounding like a smarmy used car salesman. You can promote yourself well without actually sounding like a self-promoter.

This whole word-of-mouth thing works best if you're known for doing a good job. Then your reputation spreads itself. "Everyone is so excited to have someone in the Washington, D.C., area that can do what I do that they just pass my name around," notes Alex Kramer, the private investigator. "It's a good tool for them. There's always a friend in another firm somewhere who calls them up and asks them if they know anyone good here. If they're calling me from a big investigating service to do subcontracting work, they all want someone who has done that kind of thing before because experienced people know what kind of work is expected. They say I have a monopoly on the D.C. area now." Of course if she were to burn any of them with some sloppy work, you can bet that all of her customers would hear about that pretty quickly too.

Once the word's out, you never can tell what sort of highly

placed people might hear about your business and give it a boost. At Bliss, Marcia Kilgore tends to the pores of Uma Thurman and Julia Roberts, among others. "Celebrities are just like everyone else," she says. "They want to go someplace young and fun but where they also do a good job and treat you like a normal human being. The room doesn't get all quiet and no one whispers when Uma comes in, and she has to pay like everyone else." Of course, celebrities also make great Bliss customers, since they need to tend to their looks more than most people. And when fashion magazines want to know how Uma keeps her skin so clear, she talks about Bliss and it becomes a great piece of publicity for the spa.

One of the best ways to spread the word about anything these days is through the Internet. This can be as simple as just dropping your company's name while chatting in newsgroups. "In the beginning, we just went to alt.music.wanted.cds, and when anyone said they were looking for some particular album in a record store and couldn't find it, we'd just tell them that we had it at CDNow," Jason Olim recalls. "This was when you still got flamed for spamming commercial messages all over the place, so we tried to be good citizens. But we were answering their questions. They wanted to know how to find something, and we had what they were looking for."

A good Web site will help people hear about your company, even if they aren't necessarily looking for you in particular. "When job seekers were going on the Web, they were punching in things like Goldman Sachs, and early on, a lot of those kinds of companies didn't have any Web site at all," says Gary Alpert of Wet Feet Press, the company that provides insider guides for people seeking jobs in big companies. "So we were the only thing that would pop up. We started to get quite a bit of traffic from that, and once we learned to tweak our company profiles a bit, we were able to manipulate the Web search engines into picking our site more often." Even though most large companies have recruiting Web sites today, Wet Feet's site still shows up when job seekers go hunting for general information about their target. Because the names of Wet Feet's featured companies show up prominently on the Wet Feet home page, the search engines pick it up when job hunters enter, say, Intel, into the search field thinking they're going to get the Intel home page.

In addition to providing low-cost word of mouth, Wet Feet's site also saved the company a ton of money on paper and postage. "We've never had a huge brochure," Alpert says. "We didn't have any money to print them at first, so we would just tell people to look at our Web site to see what company profiles we had available. But by the time we had enough money to think about brochures, we realized that no brochure could do a better job than the site, because on the Web you can update things constantly."

Because Kevin Donlin draws 70 percent of his résumé business off the Web, he knew he had to think creatively about how to get people to his site. Buying ads on the sites of others that will lead viewers to your site is always an option, but it can get very expensive. In Donlin's case it didn't make sense anyhow. "I am selling something that is painful for people to think about," he says, noting how anxious people become when they're looking for a new job. "It's like selling coffins. Nobody goes looking for coffin ads when they need one."

So for Donlin, the trick was trading links with other career-related sites; anyone in the recruiting area was fair game, and he wrote to many of the good sites to offer to link his site to theirs if they would do the same. The public libraries in the Twin Cities had job pages on their Web sites, and they linked to Guaranteed Resumes. Donlin also wrote some short how-to articles on résumé and cover letter writing for a few sites in exchange for links back to his own.

PASS IT ON

Offline, there are other clever ways to spread the word about your company without spending a lot of money. First, if you're aiming your wares exclusively, or even partially, at the collegiate market, don't forget that cheap labor is available to you right on campus. "Sometimes we would just grab people who were calling us on the phone to order a report on a company," says Wet Feet Press's Alpert. "We'd offer to give them the reports for free if they agreed to stuff flyers in all the mailboxes on campus for us. It helps to have a good product, because then customers are willing to go to bat for you. We've even had people volunteer to be our campus reps and sell at their schools for us. We've sold hundreds of reports on some campuses that way, and we just give those volunteers commissions for whatever they could unload."

Stuffing boxes is only one way to use a two-cent photocopy to draw business. "There are a lot of ways to use brochures and flyers that don't involve postage," says Chris Schmick, co-owner of Upper Limits, the rock-climbing gym. "We've got our brochures at hotels and the local real estate agencies, and we give them out to college and high school kids. We do birthday parties too, so we'll send all the party guests home with information for their parents in case the kids want to come back."

GIVE IT AWAY AND GET RICH

If you're producing a product that's relatively cheap, sometimes simply giving it away will draw new customers. "It doesn't feel like you're spending cash, even though you basically are," notes Tom Scott of Nantucket Nectars. "But I just remember being 12 years old and someone handing me a free cup of Colombo yogurt. I've been a Colombo guy ever since. Why? It was pretty simple. Someone gave it to me, I liked it, and there you go. Our theory is that if someone's first experience with our product is not with their eyes or their ears but their tongue, then we can get that person to be a paying customer." Nantucket Nectars now sends employees on the road full-time to pour free cups of juice at street fairs, road races, music festivals, and college campuses.

Better yet, why not pay some bribes, if you know it will lead to you snaring customers whom you wouldn't have found otherwise? "I pay a $10 referral bounty for every new client that my current clients bring me," says Guaranteed Resumes's Kevin Donlin. "It's a bargain. Right now, when you divide the cost of a Yellow Pages ad by the number of people it's bringing in each month, it's anywhere from $30 to $60 per customer. So I'm happy to send out those checks. Eventually, I'll reach a critical mass of 500 to 1,000 customers referring people to me, and I may not even need the Yellow Pages anymore."

Donlin also caught on early to the strategy of sending special notices and offering discounts to people who have used his services most often. "It's more than just a $75 résumé," he explains. "You have to think about a customer's potential lifetime value if you can keep them around. I'm happy to send out a mailing every quarter just to keep in touch with them."

ABSOLUTELY, POSITIVELY GUARANTEED

As the name of Donlin's business attests, he does guarantee his work. This doesn't cost very much, even allowing for the occasional disaster. But it does send an incredibly powerful message. "It's your saving grace on the Internet," he says. "It's a faceless environment there, since I can't meet a lot of my clients. So I keep hammering away at them, insisting that if they don't like the work I've done, I'll revise it or refund their money." So how do they know that he won't just disappear? "On the Internet, we're all publishers, and if they're not happy, they can tell the whole world that Guaranteed Resumes stiffed them. If that happens, I'm out of business. So I can't have any unhappy customers. In that way, it's actually safer for them to use me than their local Yellow Pages service, so the Internet has helped me in that respect." So far, he's only had to give out one refund.

Since the Gardner brothers don't offer a product per se on the Motley Fool—just advice that people can choose to read or ignore—it's harder to offer a guarantee. Early on, however, they decided to put their money where their mouths were and set up a model stock portfolio based on their investment philosophy. That way, readers could see that their approach actually made some sense. "Once you do that, the world becomes an absolute meritocracy. If you perform, you win. That's the way life should be," says David Gardner. If only other investment advisers were so bold. "It shouldn't have anything to do with whether you are old enough or good-looking enough. It should be: are you good?" Over the life of the business, their "foolish" portfolio has done roughly twice as well as the major stock market index groups, proving just how good the brothers are.

REMEMBER YOUR MANNERS

Finally, once you snare some loyal customers, don't forget to say thank you once in a while. "We send out thank you notes every time someone comes in for a treatment," says Bliss's Marcia Kilgore. "Everyone who comes here could choose to go someplace else next week, so we should let them know that they're appreciated. Think about it: when was the last time you got a thank you note from a business? People actually call me up to thank me for sending them a thank you note. All you get in the mail is bills and crap, so it's nice that someone has taken time out to remember you. It's not even smart. It's just manners."

AD TIME

In some businesses, it's hard to avoid having to actually pay to advertise your product. Especially in established, competitive industries, it's often a necessary evil. That doesn't mean you need to have a fancy ad agency or a big ad budget, though. Just make sure your ads show up where most of your potential customers will go looking for them, and don't waste your money on anything else. Kevin Donlin's one-eighth page Yellow Pages display ad costs him $250 per month, but it brings in about 70 customers annually. At Clementine, Elizabeth Burke and Abby Messitte pay $1,000 each year to be listed in the guide that shoppers use when they want to spend a whole day or a weekend touring galleries. It's a one-shot deal and it draws foot traffic that would never find them otherwise since the gallery isn't on street level. And all it took to get the phones at MacTemps to start ringing off the hook was one ad in the right niche publication. "You didn't buy just any computer, so why hire just any temp to run it?" they asked readers of the Boston Computer Society's newsletter. Nobody had a real good answer, so they all called MacTemps.

With juice, it's a little more complicated since there's no specialized publication that people turn to when they're thirsty. By 1996, Nantucket Nectars was expanding aggressively into new states, so Tom First and Tom Scott figured that it might make sense to do some radio ads on stations that drew the kind of young, iconoclastic listeners that would appreciate their juice. Finding the right stations was easy enough, since they all provide lots of demographic data on their listeners to anyone interested in advertising with them. But the partners didn't want the ads to sound like, well, ads. "Our product is really just the story of who we are and why we started doing this," says First. "It would be hard for an ad agency to understand it as well as we do, and what agency would want to come in and let us do it exactly the way we want to? They'd want to change things. So we produce the ads ourselves. We just go into the studio and ad lib." Which means they save a lot of money, in addition to producing ads that are incredibly distinctive.

PUBLICITY: MORE IMPACT, LESS COST

While you can spend untold amounts of money on ads, the best media of all is still free media. Sure, you have a lot less control when you're in the hands of some reporter. But the strange irony of the world of commercials has always been that companies pay lots of money to make nice ads and tons more to place them while most viewers simply tune them out. So not only will people pay better attention to your story if it's actually on the news or in the articles in the newspaper, but you also don't have to pay the reporters to get in their stories as you would for a commercial or a print ad. Plus, you'll have credibility, since it won't just be you tooting your own horn.

So how much impact can some good press actually have? Well, a lot of people read the newspaper each day, and they tend to remember interesting stories for a really long time. "In early 1993, the *Boston Globe* did a story about us," recalls Tom Scott. "It's only a regional newspaper, but a big body of people who were important to us read it each day. The retailers, bankers, consumers, and other publicity outlets all saw it. It gave us a level of credibility that we didn't have before. And it's amazing that four years later people still meet us and talk about how they just read some story about us in the *Globe*."

Even if people don't see the clip when it appears, nothing's stopping you from making 500 copies and sending it out to everyone you want to do business with. Rob Brandagee and Ava DeMarco used this strategy to get their products into new stores. No matter how good a salesperson you are, it always helps if someone else has anointed you as an Interesting Person to Watch. Sure, media people are just as clueless as everyone else when it comes to figuring out which businesses will work and which won't. But they've got the power to reach lots of people instantly, and you probably don't.

So how can you make yourself seem interesting to the people who do stories about small businesses? It actually makes a lot more sense to start off by talking about what doesn't work. As a journalist for *Fortune* magazine, I've been on the receiving end of way too many phone calls from people who have absolutely no idea how to pitch a story, and it doesn't take much to avoid some of their dumb mistakes.

First of all, put yourself in the journalist's shoes for a second and imagine you're about to be pitched for the tenth time that day. What would it take to convince you to read letters from strangers touting their business or listen to a cold call? "There are a few simple rules," says Dave Hirschkop of Dave's Gourmet. "First, think of their readers' perspective and not your own." Why do people read the publication you're trying to get your company mentioned in? If they're retailers looking for new products, then they might want to know about Dave's Gourmet's new flavored mayonnaise. The first three letters in the word *news* are *new.* But those retailers don't have time to read a feature story about all the funny calls Dave gets from people who get sick from eating too much Insanity Sauce. That would probably be a better pitch for the humor column that appears in the bottom left-hand corner of the front page of the "Marketplace" section of the *Wall Street Journal* every day. Get the idea?

"I try to work on the reporter's time frame and not ours," Hirschkop adds. Journalists at daily newspapers don't have time to wait around for you to get off the other line or return from lunch. Carry a pager or get a cell phone or check your messages every half hour, but don't ever miss a chance to get free publicity. Then, once you get on the phone, be informative, hysterical, and brief. Every journalist loves a witty, quotable sound bite, and if you can provide good ones, they'll call on you again.

In addition to being useful, it's also a good idea to take your own calls. Geek Squad's Robert Stephens asked me, "How does it make you feel when you put in a call to someone who runs a business and they have their public relations department or their assistant call you back?" (By the way, when I first called him to try to set up an interview for this book, he was out of the office but somehow managed to get back to me 30 seconds after I left a message.) "I would venture to guess that somewhere inside of you you have a little bit of contempt for the person you were originally trying to reach. . . . I want the first impression that I give people to be, 'Wow, they are fucking serious.' Sure, I totally cater to the media. But I don't kiss ass. I'm just straight with people because I'm guessing that most of the time when they're dealing with other businesses that they have to put up with a lot of waiting and bullshit."

Soon after Geek Squad was born, it began to acquire something of a cult following. Stephens had T-shirts and watches made with the company logo and gave them away freely to customers or just about anyone who asked for one. A woman at a conference happened to be wearing one of the watches and met Tom Petzinger, a *Wall Street Journal* columnist. When he asked her about her watch and heard her tell the Geek Squad story, he immediately called Stephens to arrange a visit.

Getting a journalist to talk to you, or even to come and visit, is only half the battle, though. If you don't get them excited about you and your company, then they won't be particularly inspired to turn around and tell a great story to their readers. "We really went the extra mile when Petzinger came," Stephens recalled. "We had a fleet of six Geekmobiles waiting for him at the airport."

After the story in the *Journal, People* magazine called to do a feature story. "The photographer came up from Chicago, and his name was Lewis Toby," Stephens says. "So I stood there at the airport with two guys in their black suits with a blackboard that said 'Dr. Lewis Toby, Helsinki Polytechnic Institute' on it. He just about peed in his pants. There were two of our ice cream trucks there, and we loaded all his equipment in the back, and then put him in the back of my Simca. So what do we have to gain by giving this guy the time of his life? He's going to take the best fucking pictures he has ever taken. Because he wants to. Because he's turned on by all this."

So let's say you don't have a Geekmobile or a clip-on tie. What types of stories are also likely to make an impression on journalists? Fortunately, the epic of the upstart start-up is one that never loses its appeal (how do you think I sold this book to Broadway?). Everyone's curious about brash young people with great ideas, whether it's investors hoping to get in on the ground floor of the next big idea or people like you who are trying to figure out how to do it yourself. So there's no need to be shy about it. "We've been called the Gallery Girls, the Gen X Gallery Girls, or just the Clementine Girls," says Clementine's Abby Messitte, noting that it's not that bad to still be a girl at age 26 if it's not meant to be degrading or derogatory. Just as long as people are talking about you.

It's also smart to keep a close eye on what's happening in the news. You may think you have better things to do than keep up with the world when you're also putting in 100 hours each week to keep your business afloat, but good publicity opportunities come and go in a flash, so it's important to be aware of them. Doug Chu and Scott Samet, who own Taste of Nature and distribute healthy snacks to movie theaters, were watching the papers when a big study came out in 1995 trashing movie theater popcorn. "The business was two years old when that story hit, and at the time, we were the only ones in the game focusing on healthy snacks," Samet says. "We made a million phone calls and faxes, just working the PR circuit as hard as we could. Within a few months, we had been on NBC, one of the morning news shows, "E!," the cover of the *L.A. Business Journal,* and in *Forbes,* the *L.A. Times,* and the *Orange County Register."* Sure, they got lucky with the timing of that survey, but it wouldn't have done them any good if they hadn't heard about it in the first place and jumped on it the way that they did. While several theater chains sold Taste of Nature products at that point, the amazing publicity blitz opened many more doors for the company.

Of course it doesn't hurt to create the news yourself. Dave Hirschkop has gotten a lot of media mileage out of the fact that his product was kicked out of the National Fiery Foods Show because his Insanity Sauce was too hot. And Kevin Donlin of Guaranteed Resumes writes articles himself, hoping that the little tag line at the end of his clips identifying him as the owner of a résumé-writing service will draw new business. "I write for magazines, the local weekly employment publication, and I post the articles on my Web site too, so people can pick them up that way as well," Donlin says.

MOUTHS FOR HIRE

Like Donlin, most of the young entrepreneurs I've mentioned have generated their own buzz by writing letters and making phone calls themselves. Like most things in life, however, plenty of people out there will do this sort of thing for you, for a price. Having done this before for other clients, public relations firms will probably have better media contacts than you. If this pays off with a higher success rate than you would have on your own, then it's probably worth spending some money to hire one.

There are a lot of public relations firms in the world, and many of them do totally half-assed work. How do you find one that won't? "We were at a trade show, and we asked some people from another company that we respected who they used," recalls Little Earth's Rob Brandagee. "They had hired a guy who they said was tremendous and focused specifically on environmental issues, which was important to us since we make most of our stuff from recycled products. We put him on the budget long before we could really afford to, but we thought he could get us the kind of credibility that would get us into major department stores."

"PR is a lot of work," adds Brandagee's partner, Ava DeMarco. "You're sending out press releases and following each one up with a phone call. We had always talked about doing more of it at the graphic design firm where I used to work, but we never got around to it there. I finally realized that if we didn't hire a professional to do it at Little Earth, it would never get done. You tend to think that your time is worthless when you start a business, but it isn't. There's only so much time in the day, so you should spend as much of it as possible doing the things that you're really good at." Since neither of them knew much about public relations, they scraped together the $1,200 a month they needed to put the guy they'd heard about on retainer. Within a year, they and their products had been on television a few dozen times and appeared in tons of magazines and newspapers, including a major feature in the *Wall Street Journal*. "That alone was worth the money we spent on him," DeMarco says now.

If you can't afford to pay as much as Little Earth did to hire a pro, don't despair. Plenty of young entrepreneurs in public relations may be willing to cut you a deal and will probably be hungrier than someone twice your age. "I knew some people from college who had just started their own firm," says Julia Stern of Malia

Mills. "They took us on for free, because they figured that they could get us some good press fairly easily and then use the success they'd had with us to lure paying clients in the future. It was basically just two needy companies using each other to promote themselves."

In fact, you may always get better work from the small firms, and this isn't just true in public relations but also in law firms, accounting practices, and others. The big firms have already proven themselves, and they'll probably save their best people for their biggest clients. Smaller firms have more on the line, so the big brains are likely to be paying more attention to clients like you with smaller companies. Besides, what goes around comes around. If all the upstart start-ups in the world were to feed each other business, everyone would have a better chance of lasting for the long haul.

CHAPTER 7

THE NUTS AND BOLTS

Turning Your Idea into an Operation

One of the most exciting—and most frightening—things that can happen to any business is for the marketing to work too well. People are so impressed by what they're hearing about or seeing from you that their demand for your product or services strains your capacity to provide it because you don't yet have the firepower to churn it out. I know, I know—we should all have such problems. But seriously, for your business to make money, you need to have someplace to run it out of, enough inventory on hand to meet demand, and the right selection of it. Then, you need to know how to communicate with your customers, charge prices that make sense, and have a system to keep track of what you're selling. It's somewhat akin to blocking and tackling in football; it's pretty basic stuff, but you can't win any games unless you do it well every day.

LICENSED TO SELL

First of all, you may need permission from the government to exist. Different industries have different requirements, and even those will differ from state to state and city to city. In general, though, if you're doing anything that has to do with food, there will be some licensing involved. If liquor is in the mix, figure on having tons of paperwork to deal with. Todd Alexander of Vendemmia even had to deal with the federal government. "I walked into the Atlanta office of the Bureau of Alcohol, Tobacco, and Firearms and told them what I was trying to do, and they gave me a stack of forms about a mile high," he recalls. "Over the years, this industry hasn't drawn the most savory people, and enterprises like mine have been used to launder money. So when a 25-year-old black guy comes in wanting to get a license, well, I don't know what they were thinking. But every time I came back with my forms, they had more questions for me. All I knew was that my record was clean, and I was just, like, could you please give me my license so I can get on with my life?" It took nine months for Alexander to get the go-ahead from Uncle Sam, so keep that in mind if you need permission from the government before you open up.

CORNER OFFICES

In addition to getting permission to exist, you'll also need a place to set up shop. In the beginning, the path of least resistance is generally to just start your business out of your home. If your own apartment is too small, you might even end up running it out of your parents' home. "I'll always remember when the guys came into my mother's house to install the T1 line for our high-speed Internet connection," says Jason Olim of CDNow. "They looked at her and asked, 'Did *you* order this?' They came in with thousands of dollars worth of equipment, she showed them to the basement, and they shoved all the wiring behind the old wood paneling down there."

This sort of thing can work well for a while. The American basement, the archetypal garage—these spots have a hallowed place in the annals of U.S. business history since they're the birthplace of Apple, Hewlett-Packard, and so many other companies. Cramped quarters have a tendency to infuse everything with a skunkworks mentality, with lots of busy people huddled over work in small spaces. No start-up should have a real office anyway, right?

But you'll be surprised at how quickly all that romanticism will wear off once you get over yourself. The garage, the basement, or your apartment will soon feel less like the birthplace of the next Microsoft and more like the one-room triple that college freshmen have to share. "Steve and I started in a one-bedroom apartment, where he was living on a pullout sofa in the living room, which doubled as the office," recalls Wet Feet Press's Gary Alpert. "Eventually, we graduated to a two-bedroom. His bedroom was the office, and the living room became the order fulfillment area. I'd be off doing consulting projects to make ends meet, and he'd be there answering phones, giving interviews to college newspapers, and doing everything else. He couldn't get his writing done."

Steve eventually moved out, but it didn't end the space crunch.

"I had seven phone lines, but eventually we had about 14 people working there," Alpert says. "The landlord didn't want me installing any more lines, so I had to rent an extra room upstairs and run them in through the window."

While this setup may sound amusing, it can severely impede your employees' ability to get work done. "People were willing to tolerate too much," Alpert continues. "Our computers crashed all the time because we couldn't get the right kind of network going in that space, but people didn't want to complain, so they wouldn't come to us to say that they couldn't get their work done because they couldn't get e-mail for two hours." Indeed, everyone will try to be a good sport about these sorts of things, but people's patience lasts only so long. You'll be able to keep better employees for a longer period of time if you don't put them through that sort of thing. Not to mention that you'll have no life if all these people are working at your house all the time. Wet Feet Press eventually found office space in the South of Market neighborhood of San Francisco.

Even if you don't have a whole bunch of employees right away, you're bound to draw unwanted attention to yourself if you're running, say, a factory out of your house. "We lived on a quiet dead-end street, and every day, the UPS truck would block the whole thing," recalls Rob Brandagee, who started Little Earth out of the house that he shared with Ava DeMarco in Pittsburgh. "It obviously wasn't zoned for that sort of thing. I would drag the stamping machine out in the driveway when it was nice outside, which kind of made a lot of noise. By the time we were politely asked to leave by the neighbors who had had enough, the business had taken over the whole house. We were making belts in our bedroom."

Finding your own space doesn't have to be expensive. Little Earth ended up in a reconditioned factory building in a run-down section of town that rented out for next to nothing. Malia Mills and Julia Stern sublet part of their space in Manhattan's flower district to reduce their costs. And Wet Feet Press landed in their San Francisco neighborhood just as rents exploded; by leasing an entire floor and parceling some of it out to other companies at a higher rate per square foot than they're paying themselves, they've actually saved a lot of money.

SO HOW CAN I GET 5,000 OF THESE THINGS, PRONTO?

Even if you have your back office in order, you've got to figure out where your products are going to come from. For every item that already exists, there are bound to be a number of distributors or middlemen out there hoping to sell it to you at wholesale prices, so you can then turn around and sell it to your customers at a profit. But if you're planning on selling something that you've invented—something entirely new—you're going to have to find a way to make it from scratch. Needless to say, this sort of thing can get pretty complicated.

There are basically two ways to go: hire a factory to make your products for you, or put one together yourself. Kate Spade chose the first option when it came time to assemble her handbags, but first she had to show the people at the factory what to make and deliver them the materials to make it with. "I didn't have any idea what to do at all," she recalls. "I didn't have the slightest clue about where to get fabric, how to make patterns, or who would make the labels and sell me the zippers. I tried a lot of things that didn't work. I looked up 'Sewing' in the Yellow Pages. I rang doorbells in Chinatown in New York, where a lot of the garment factories are."

This scattershot approach didn't amount to much at first. A better approach is to employ something that Dave Hirschkop refers to as the "up the river, down the river" strategy. When he wanted to know who could bottle his hot sauce for him, he figured it might make sense to look upstream and ask the people who make the bottles, figuring they would know which of their customers bottled hot sauce and which bottled mouthwash. The founders of Nantucket Nectars called everyone from a winery to Ocean Spray to see what they could glean about the bottling process.

Andy and Kate Spade caught on to this notion quickly, and soon she was calling friends in the lingerie business and contacts from her days as an accessories editor at *Mademoiselle* to find the help she needed. "Someone told me that you can hire a pattern maker to do the actual blueprints for your bags by looking at the ads in *Women's Wear Daily,* so that was easy," she says. "Once I started going to these factories and fabric companies, though, most people wouldn't take me seriously. One guy told me later that he didn't think I would pay because I had a hole in my sweater. I think a lot of students come in planning to manufacture things but never actually go through with it."

Spade was persistent, however, and managed to manipulate the system to get what she needed. "Most people won't sell you less than 1,000 yards of fabric per color, but bags don't use that much fabric, and we were just starting, so there was no way we could use that much," she says. "They would give out a small amount of sample yardage to make a prototype for a trade show, though. So I would use different names with the same people and actually get enough sample yardage to do all our production runs because they were so small at first." Using similar wiliness, she turned up one or two factories that would sew the bags. As the company's production runs grew larger, it became easier to negotiate better deals.

Though Spade had to spend lots of time in rough parts of town trying to get her bags made, at least she was manufacturing a product that manufacturers were familiar with. Magnetized poetry squares didn't exist before Dave Kapell invented them, so trying to find someone to make Magnetic Poetry's products was an even tougher challenge. "At first, I was going to the office supply store and getting these little kits that people could use to magnetize their business cards," he recalls. "So I would print the words out from the computer and paste them on to the magnet strips and then cut them out. It got slightly more advanced when I began hiring my friends and family to do piecework. I even bought them all paper cutters."

But as the product grew into a full-fledged phenomenon, Kapell knew he needed to figure out a way to mass produce his poetry kits. Like Spade, he figured that the fastest way to do it would be to hire somebody else who knew more about it all than he did. "I just looked in the Yellow Pages under 'Screen Printing' and 'Die Cutting,' " he recalls. "There were four places that sounded like they could do what I needed, so I got in my car one day and visited all of them. At the first two places, the guys I met were total assholes. I probably should have dressed up more, but I figured that I was a potential customer so it wouldn't be an issue. All they wanted to know was how I was going to be able to pay them."

Though Kapell had enough cash to pay for a small run at first, he knew that eventually he would need credit from these people, and he didn't like the way he was being treated. "At both places, it was older guys that I had met with, and they were really unpleasant and condescending," he says. "When I went to the third one, though, I met with a guy who was about my age. I could tell he was sort of an upstart trying to be a success on his own, and I could see that he understood immediately what I was trying to do."

As Amy Nye Wolf learned when she first approached the airport authority to pitch the Altitunes concept, it always helps if you can find a decision maker who's young enough to understand where you are in life and how hungry you are to make your idea work. Kapell's sales rep at the third die cutter talked the shop's controller into giving Kapell credit right away. "It was a scary agreement, basically saying that they would own my company if I didn't pay them in 90 days," he recalls. "But I had to bet the farm, because the economies of scale on all of this were so large. It probably costs the same to make 10,000 kits as it does to make 5,000, since so much of the work is simply in setting up the equipment to do this. So it didn't make financial sense to do smaller runs, but I didn't have the cash to pay for a larger one."

For those who are truly brave, there's that second big production option, which is to build a factory from scratch. If you're a company like Little Earth, making everything from bags to belts to notebooks, you may have no choice but to do it yourself. First of all, most places won't produce small batches of goods, but you may not have the cash to order a large production run. Also, no one factory was going to be able to produce everything that Little Earth wanted to make, and trying to juggle contracts with several manufacturers would have been a lot to deal with for a small company. So Rob Brandagee and Ava DeMarco set out to do it all themselves.

Most of Little Earth's products don't require a lot of high-tech production. They just need some cutting, sewing, and fastening, and that could be done with a few large machines that they were able to buy and park in the cavernous space they had leased on the cheap. The real issue was finding sources for their raw materials: the bottle caps to fasten to their belts, the license plates that were turned into notebooks, and the used rubber from tires that they use in several products.

"Every vacation we take, we spend at least part of it in the local junkyards," DeMarco says. "We stopped at one on the way to the airport in Hawaii once, and we almost missed our flight because we found these big boxes of license plates that we wanted." Once the company had established relationships with the dealers who save this sort of stuff, they no longer had to hang around the trash heaps as much. "There are just a few big dealers, and they all know one another, so once they find out that you're buying, they come to you with product. We're now the largest purchaser of used license plates in the country."

For other items, the trick has been to convince people to save things that they might otherwise throw out. "We have buckets in every bar in Pittsburgh that say 'Help Little Earth recycle bottlecaps,' " Brandagee explains. "We come around and pick them up every so often, and we give the bartenders coupons for merchandise depending on how much they've saved." So not only is the company keeping these things from filling up landfills, they're getting their raw materials for next to nothing. That's no small matter when they're going through about four million bottlecaps each year to make their belts. (In case you're keeping track, by the way, that's about 12 beers annually for every legal drinker in Pittsburgh. And that's only counting the caps that get saved.)

NOW WHAT WERE WE SELLING AGAIN?

Once you start churning out product in large quantities, you'll have to start testing it in the market. For real this time. Surprisingly, often the first things that change radically once a new business opens up are the product offerings themselves. While all that market research you did was probably helpful, once you have real customers you'll begin to see what you missed while planning your business in the abstract.

For instance, as mentioned in chapter 2, John Chuang's storefront computer rental business that he and his Harvard classmates were so proud of was only a treasure map that led to MacTemps, which today is a $106 million business. Much of Robert Stephens's background was in constructing the circuits for flight simulators at the University of Minnesota; originally, he thought that the Geek Squad would work exclusively for NASA. Both Chuang and Stephens eventually figured out who their best customers were likely to be, and Stephens gave up his dream of working on spaceships. But neither of them figured this out until after they had been open for business for a while.

The changes may not be so dramatic, of course. Sometimes it just involves the tweaking of your product mix. "There's a certain insecurity that comes from selling only one product. If that stops, your company stops," notes Dave Hirschkop, who built Dave's Gourmet on the strength of his Insanity Sauce. "Besides, the stuff was so hot that one bottle might last a whole year. While there aren't that many products that have the potential to sell 20 or 30 million units each year, I knew that at least I had to do something other than just hot sauce." Today, Dave sells flavored mayonnaise, beef jerky, hot jellybeans, and pickles, among other food products.

When Amy Nye Wolf opened her first Altitunes store in New York's La Guardia Airport, she realized that there was no reason why she couldn't sell portable CD players along with the CDs. And given that people are often traveling to see their families, she eventually decided to try video cameras too. "We get a ton of movie stars and celebrities and other superwealthy people who are passing through," Wolf says. "These people are impulse shoppers. They don't make price comparisons first. That's not to say that we're ripping them off, but we're clearly not the best deal in town. And all we have to do is sell a couple of them a week for it to have a big impact on our overall sales." It also helps that profit margins on consumer electronics are about twice what they are for compact discs.

BIRTH OF A SALESMAN

Unfortunately, Wolf has to rely on more than impulse shoppers to make money, and so will you. It would be nice if your goods just flew out of the store once you figured out how to make them and have a place to put them. It would be great if you started a service business (which is even better because you don't need to produce any "goods" up front) where everyone just flocks to your door and you don't have to lift a finger to get them there. Good products will help, and great marketing will too, but sooner or later, you, the creative genius, are going to have to roll up your sleeves and politely beg people to bring you their business. You're going to have to play salesperson.

For many businesses, the biggest challenge is to get into enough retail outlets in the first place. If you're not selling your product or service yourself, you have to literally sell yourself to stores first before they'll put your product out on their shelves. "You may be able to get into the boutiques," notes Andy Spade, "but it's much harder when you're dealing with a chain that has 50 stores. They see you out there, but they want to know that you are financially secure and well managed enough to get your product to them on time. With a company our size, it was a real big risk for them to take us on." Indeed, if the company hadn't delivered their first big orders on time, a lot of department stores would have been left with empty shelves. After all, no store has the time or money to order backup inventory just in case one of their suppliers drops the ball.

On top of this, some retailers and wholesalers don't believe that someone your age can or will deliver on your promises. You simply may not be able to win some of those people over, just as Dave Kapell and Kate Spade couldn't convince some potential suppliers that they were serious.

It also helps if you can make a simple appeal to sound business logic, which is how Taste of Nature got its healthy snacks into movie theaters. "We focused on incremental sales and profit margins," says cofounder Scott Samet. "This was a product that would appeal to people who weren't buying any concessions at all. It wasn't going to cannibalize the M&M's. Plus, the profit margins were higher than they were for things like Häagen-Dazs ice cream bars, so theater operators could make more money selling our product." Samet and his partner, Doug Chu, say they've never felt like age has been an obstacle that they've had to clear.

The fact that they picked the right retailers from day one

helped too. Having lots of people hawking your product doesn't mean much if it costs *you* money to sell to 90 percent of them. Instead of chasing independent theater operators with a couple movie theaters, Taste of Nature aimed most of its early sales pitches at the largest chains, which can efficiently sell a lot more snacks.

The overall size and profitability of the potential customer base obviously matters a lot, but so do the demographics of the potential customers. "If you're trying to run up your sales right away, Wal-Mart is a great place to sell your goods," says Julia Stern of Malia Mills swimwear. "But if you're trying to build a particular kind of brand, you may be better off staying away from stores like that." This is not snobbishness, though it may sound like it. It's simply a matter of choosing a design philosophy and then aiming it at the market niche that will appreciate it most.

If you're aiming at the higher end of the market, as both Malia Mills and Kate Spade were, it pays to be patient while you build a name for yourself. "It's hard to build a business when you're not going for volume right away," notes Andy Spade. "For something like this, though, it makes sense to try to attract a cult following in the beginning. We tried to get opinion leaders and fashion insiders to carry the bags early on." They even declined to allow some large, upscale department stores to carry the bags at first. "If the bags are everywhere," says Kate Spade, "no one will really want them."

Admittedly, this strategy applies only to certain industries, although the fashion business has traditionally been open to a lot of young upstarts. Another sales strategy that involves the careful targeting of customers is to simply aim at those who spend the most money. That's who Kevin Donlin aimed his marketing at and that's who Elizabeth Burke and Abby Messitte are betting on to push Clementine Gallery into profitability. While it's nice if they can talk a couple dozen twentysomethings into buying a $500 piece of art each month, the real money is in getting hard-core collectors to come in and buy things repeatedly.

Unfortunately, this was a lesson that the Clementine partners learned the hard way. "There's a whole protocol about dealing with serious collectors. They like to be coddled and have their hands held. They expect it. And we didn't know about that," says Messitte. Burke continues: "I guess you're supposed to know who they are when they pass through, because it's not like they stop and say, 'Hi, I'm so and so.' They expect you to know who they are and kiss their ass. I would do it. Shit, if it's going to save my business, it's no skin off my back. But we didn't know that, and even if we did, they don't have 'collector' written on their forehead."

So how did they figure it out? "One guy called who is an advisor to collectors," Messitte says. "He takes them around and shows them interesting work that they might want to consider. He wanted to come in when we were closed, and we couldn't do it because we both have other jobs. He was pissed, and we found out he was going around town saying that those girls don't know how to run a business." Needless to say, the two partners bent over backwards to make amends and have made it their business to learn who the collectors about town are.

A little unbridled enthusiasm has never cost anyone a sale. "If you can get people excited about something, they'll want to believe that you know what you're doing," says Bliss's Marcia Kilgore. "When I first got started, I may not have been the best facialist around, but I was the most enthusiastic about doing it for people. Customers can sense that, and when they do, they want what you have to offer and won't get it from somebody else. I mean, when I clean out people's pores, I go at it for an hour if I need to. I've tried a lot of the competition, and a lot of the time I come home with the same blackheads I had when I looked in the mirror that morning."

Still, some potential customers may make themselves totally inaccessible at first, so it's important to be clever in finding ways to reach them. "Race plays a role, so I'm not eager to go out and call on every possible account in the city," says Todd Alexander of Vendemmia. "I know what the dynamics are. Just because I have great wine doesn't mean that people [in some of the all-white counties] are going to let me call on them." Alexander has gotten around this problem by hiring white sales reps to grow his business in certain regions.

But that's just the side of Alexander's business where he has to move the product out. He also has to convince the wineries to let him sell their wares in the first place. The vineyard owners generally pick just one distributor to work with in Georgia and then sign an exclusive agreement with that one firm. "There are two kinds of wineries," he explains. "There are the people who are in it simply to move as many boxes as possible, so in that case I take a deep breath and puff myself up to explain how a small distributor can still do big business with the large retail accounts that can do special promotions. Then there are the small wineries, where more ego is involved. They want to be in the best stores and best restaurants, so in that case I emphasize that we're small enough to pay attention to them and place their wines in the right locations. Without lying, you have to tell both kinds of wineries exactly what they want to hear."

Getting in the front door to talk is only the first half of your selling task. Learning when to go in for the kill and when to back off has been another lesson that Burke and Messitte have taught themselves on the fly. "One thing I've learned to do is not to trust that people will call me in a week if they say they're interested in coming back and looking at something again," Burke says. "I don't let them walk out of the gallery without getting their business card.

"Another thing I've been working on lately is something more subtle. If a customer walks in, you always want to greet them to make some initial contact. If you say, 'Do you have any questions?' you'll almost always get a quick 'no' for an answer. But if you tell them, 'Please let me know if you have any questions,' they almost always end up asking you something. The wording makes a lot of difference."

As Burke points out, the most important thing to do when someone new shows up at your door or calls on the phone is just to try to get a conversation going. Then you can let subtle persuasion take over. "I'm surprised at what the suggestion of considering a portable CD player can do to the outcome," says Altitunes's Amy Nye Wolf, noting how many people buy CDs in the airport for their home stereo system without ever considering how nice it would be to have one on the airplane too. "No one shows up expecting to buy a Discman, but we ask them if they've ever tried one and have them try one on. People remember when they were so expensive a few years back, but now there are some for under $150. And then they end up walking away with one."

THE PRICE IS RIGHT

The price point issue is pretty important, though it's often hard to figure out just exactly what customers will consider a good deal. Take a brand new product for instance, something that has never existed before. How do you know how much to charge for it? "You don't," says Gary Alpert of Wet Feet Press. "We had a sense of what we might have paid for something like that when we were in school, but we weren't sure. The two of us have different spending habits, and much depends on how desperate someone is to work for a particular company. When we did focus groups, a lot of people said they wouldn't pay anything, and others said they would only pay about five dollars.

"When we tested out prices at business schools with the actual product, we sold them at Stanford for $15, Kellogg for $20, and Harvard for $25, just because we really wanted to stick it to Harvard. We had sales everywhere, though we sold the most at Stanford. Typically, once people had read the report they told us that they thought that the price had been cheap. So we decided to sell them for $25, though we often discount down to $15."

What if you're selling a product that people already buy, but you're delivering it in an entirely new manner? "My brother and I had a big battle over price," says CDNow's Jason Olim. "He wanted to charge the lowest price possible, but I felt like ours was a business of selection, information, and convenience. That was the way we were going to make our mark, and we had to charge enough money to be able to support that." Indeed, the only ways to sustain the lowest price strategy is if you're keeping overhead low or selling more product than anyone else and are therefore able to negotiate the best discounts with your suppliers. Of course, if you have money to burn, you can try to buy your way into a market by beating the lowest price in your industry, but how long can you sustain that? And what will happen to your customers once the inevitable happens and you have to charge them more?

The partners at Career Central for MBAs didn't face these questions at first, since they were selling a service that was different from anything that had ever been offered before. In some ways, however, that makes the pricing challenge that much more acute. "We knew what newspapers charged, and how completely ineffective they were in helping companies find most high-level employees," says Jeffrey Hyman. "We knew what it cost for companies to buy books of résumés from the business schools, which was about $300. And we knew headhunters charged somewhere between 20 and 35 percent of a new hire's first-year salary. If we charged below $1,000, we figured it would be tough to make any kind of a profit, but if we went much higher than $5,000, people would probably start lumping us in with the headhunters."

Then again, the partners had to decide exactly what customers would get in return for the money. Would Career Central get paid only if the company hired someone from its database, or were the companies just paying for the leads? Should they get all the résumés that match their needs, or should they have to pay for each one? How about asking for a big chunk of cash in return for unlimited access to the database for, say, a year? "I'm generally not a big believer in pricing research, because what they say and what they pay often don't have much in common," Hyman says. "But it did help us figure out how to charge. People want to be able to tell their boss, 'OK, this is what it's going to cost.' So we settled on the flat fee per search model, decided to charge $2,000, and did not guarantee that they would get a match. We got some resistance, but not a ton." If you don't get any people bitching and moaning about your rates, that usually means you're not charging enough, so Hyman and Yuen probably had it just about right. Eventually, they raised it to $2,995 as the job market got hotter in the late 1990s.

One way to completely differentiate yourself from your competitors is to make it very difficult for customers to comparison shop. If you think it's impossible to do this without making them feel like they're getting ripped off, consider how Robert Stephens accomplished this at Geek Squad. "In early 1997, I decided to switch to flat-rate pricing instead of adding up all these different charges on every customer's bill," Stephens explains. "So now if someone calls and wants a new hard drive installed, I can just tell them that it costs $198. When they want to know what the trip charge will be to send someone to their house, I tell them that it's still $198. If they bring it in to our office, it's still $198 but they might get it back a little faster. I actually was able to raise my effective hourly rate, but nobody knows that. Why? Because they can't compare it to the competition, which charges according to how long it takes them to get it done. I even built in a 12 percent attrition rate to my projections when I switched, but no customers had a problem with it. It's the most simple, elegant system."

One of the nicest things about flat-rate pricing is that it makes recordkeeping easier, since employees don't have to keep track of their hours. Even so, meticulousness has never been something that Stephens has lacked. "There are a lot of people out there who have better technical skills than I do but don't know shit about paperwork," he says. "It takes a real sick mind to love filing things, but I love organizing."

WATCHING YOUR PENNIES

If you're not as turned on by accounting as Stephens seems to be, you need to make sure you have an accountant or someone on staff who will be turned on for you. Nothing sinks a business faster than not knowing where the money is going or getting a visit from the IRS when you've lost track of half your income. Good numbers people can even help you earn more. "If you know how to deduct things and play it all correctly, you'll have a lot more money coming to you," says private investigator Alex Kramer. "The ignorance kind of slowed some of my growth. I didn't realize things, like the fact that there's this huge tax deduction for investing in computer equipment. It was my accountant who told me that. Until you start putting everything down on paper, it really is hard to figure out where all your money is going, where it's coming from, and where it should be going." When you're just getting started, a good computer program like Intuit's QuickBooks can help you keep track of things until you get a real pro to attack your financial statements.

One of the best reasons to keep careful track of your money is that people steal. It's easy to get lost in a burst of idealism in your first few months of being in business for yourself. While you won't succeed without that sort of optimism, you have to remember that this is the real world that you're dealing with, and people are going to try to rip you off. In fact, it's almost inevitable if you have more than a handful of people working for you. If you deal with it correctly once it does happen, however, you stand a good chance of keeping it from happening again.

"I had always figured that people wouldn't take stuff if they liked their job, but that was really dumb of me," says Altitunes's

Amy Nye Wolf. "They can look you in the eye and say that they didn't, but you know which location the inventory is disappearing from. When it happened at La Guardia, I had to just fire the whole staff and start over. They may not have all been guilty, but to this day I don't think I fired anyone who didn't deserve it. They all must have known about people taking CDs, even if they weren't actually doing it themselves. We also made sure that everyone else at all the other locations heard about it. Then we installed video cameras at every store and are prosecuting an employee we caught stealing." Today, Wolf just shrugs her shoulders and builds a certain amount of inventory "shrinkage" into her projections, but at least she's made it a lot harder for her employees to get away with it.

Your customers will find all sorts of ways to avoid paying as well, whether it's shoplifting or simply disappearing before their bill to you comes due. There are only so many things you can do to avoid this sort of thing, though Wet Feet Press has come up with a rather unique method. Its corporate guides average about 35 pages in length, and they're printed on standard-size paper. Theoretically, anyone could just buy one, shove it in a Xerox machine, and hand it out to 20 friends, thus depriving Wet Feet Press of hundreds of dollars in revenues.

Some of this undoubtedly goes on, but in the front of each report they print a few things intended to shame readers who are thinking about running off a few copies. "We basically just tell them our story, that we're two guys a lot like them, just trying to make a go of it running our own business," Alpert says. "We ask them nicely to refrain from photocopying the reports. They're not that expensive, and when people do that sort of thing it really has a tangible adverse impact on our company. Some customers have even told us that they've been at the copy machine when they read our top ten reasons not to copy Wet Feet Press reports and then decided not to. Now that said, we know that a lot of it goes on anyway, and at least it helps spread our brand name. But even with the copying, we still think we'll continue to have a large enough market of paying customers to make it all work."

The last group of people, the ones who are likely to steal from you the most, are your competitors. Todd Alexander lost two of his best employees to larger wholesalers in Atlanta. The partners at Clementine have poured their heart and soul into putting up shows for emerging artists only to have more established galleries swipe them away. But hey, it's a tough world, and unless you have patents on your products or iron-clad contracts with your people, you're basically shit out of luck.

Better to strike first then. "All our paperwork was 100 percent knocked off the temp agency I worked for before I started college," says John Chuang. "The time sheets, the phone system, everything." Adds Kevin Donlin: "I watch my competition carefully. They take my best ideas for themselves, and I take their best ideas for my own work. There's no need to reinvent the wheel on your own. That's why I just try to make my brain work like a giant piece of Velcro."

CHAPTER 8

MANAGEMENT 101

Yes, You Can Call a Meeting, Even if This Isn't IBM

One of the things that often happens when you become your own boss is that you end up being someone else's too. This probably wasn't what you had in mind when you started your company. After all, if you had had a burning desire to be in charge of hundreds of people, you would have gotten an M.B.A. and gone to work for IBM. In entrepreneurship, the need to be a good manager is generally a by-product of your success as an innovator. In other words, while you may have started a company because you wanted to find new or better ways to do business in a particular industry, the more successful you are at that, the more people you'll need to hire to help spread your gospel to new customers. Somebody's got to find them all and tell them what to do, and that task falls to those who started the company in the first place.

CONGRATULATIONS! NOW YOU'RE THE HUMAN RESOURCES DIRECTOR, TOO

So now you're a manager, and it's probably best to start any discussion of management with hiring, since it may be the most important task you'll face in the first few years of your company's life. If you do it right the first time, you'll save yourself a lot of hassle down the road because you won't have to replace all the people you had hired who didn't work out. Still, it's not easy, for with each new person you hire, you're giving up a little bit more control of your enterprise. It's sort of like putting your newborn child in the hands of a babysitter. While you have the ability to check up on the kid fairly often, you can't always keep the person who's minding the baby from making mistakes, nor can you force him or her to do things exactly the way that you would do them yourself.

The natural instinct away from delegation always begins with the cliché that says that if you want something done right, you ought to do it yourself. After all, no one cares for a business more than the person who owns it. It may be true that, early on, you're able to do everything well yourself. But eventually the overall effect on the business becomes negative if the founders are stretched so thin that they can't think straight about the big strategic issues.

Amy Nye Wolf, who picked up great financial skills during her years at Goldman Sachs, hired a chief financial officer when she had only eight Altitunes airport CD kiosks open. "I can do projections with the best of them, and I probably could have learned the accounting skills that I would have needed to continue to handle the financial side of all this myself," she says. "But I knew it was better to hire someone else to do that so I could focus on marketing and putting more stores in new airports."

So what sort of background should you look for in the people whom you're hiring early on in the life of your business? One rule of thumb is to try to hire people who are better than you at the tasks you're hiring them to do. That way, each time you bring in someone new, the company's average level of ability goes up. "My first rule of hiring has always been to bring in people who are smarter than I am for key positions like sales and marketing and then learn from them. It's the only way you're ever going to go anywhere," says CDNow's Jason Olim. "It can be kind of scary, when you realize how much more someone who works for you knows about a particular subject than you do. But the most wonderful thing about it is that they will come to you with these fully formed ideas that you never could have conceived of on your own."

Another approach is to seek out the most hungry, driven people you can possibly find, even if they are somewhat green. Then just turn them loose in their jobs. "I think we've always looked for desire and passion first before experience," says Nantucket Nectars's Tom Scott. "We hear it over and over from our retailers and others that we work with: 'Your people really care about what they are doing.' They're not commenting on their technical skills but on their ability as human beings to relate to their customers. We also do a good job of training people along those lines, not just in the X's and O's but on the overall culture of the company. Because we have a bigger group now, we're bringing 5 people into a company of 105, which means they have a lot of people to learn from. There's a tradition here now that we didn't always have."

As Scott's comments suggest, a company that's smaller than Nantucket Nectars may not be able to wean someone along in that manner. This is particularly true for jobs in finance and operations, which take a fair bit of time to learn to do well. "We tried to bring in one inexperienced person that we hoped would pick things up as quickly as we needed her to, but we were wasting our time and hers thinking we had the time to teach everything," says Kate Spade. Her husband, Andy, echoes the same point: "This was something we talked about all the time at the ad agency where I used to work. You may have no doubt that someone new could be great someday soon, but if you don't have the manpower to absorb the training process, you have to get someone who already knows what they are doing."

On the other hand, for the jobs that aren't at the top of the company's organizational chart—or for any job in sales, public relations, or customer service—a new hire's ability to imitate a giant sponge may ultimately count for more than anything else. "Our business has never been on the fast-track, five-years-and-then-go-public route," notes John Chuang of MacTemps. "We're on more of a 30-year plan, and for that kind of company, you just need to make sure that you've hired people with a fast rate of learning, so that by the time those first five years have gone by, they have the capacity to quickly learn the additional skills they'll need to get you from your fifth year to the tenth."

In other words, in many positions, brains can often take your company a lot further than a bunch of brawny résumés will. "We hire really smart people," Chuang adds. "If I have people who can keep up no matter what we do, then I have a core, a group of people who understand the company and its history. Then it's much easier to make everything else fit together."

Intelligence, of course, is just one small part of the equation when you're trying to figure out if the person across the table is someone you'll want working for you. So when Jason Olim hires new people to work at CDNow, it's their personalities that he's really trying to gauge. "In the world of the Internet, no one's all that experienced because the medium is too new," he says. "So attitude is far more important than pedigree."

This is a lesson that the owners of Little Earth learned the hard way. "If you hire someone who is an expert but is also an asshole, it's not going to do you much good," says Rob Brandagee. "We hired a sales director in the summer of 1996 because we thought we needed a big national guy who had worked in a lot of name companies," explains his partner, Ava DeMarco. "He was older, a little reserved, sort of aloof, but we thought maybe that's what we needed—a little professionalism. But his management skills turned out to be really poor. He didn't want to move to Pittsburgh, but all his staff was here, which made things difficult. And he was totally computer illiterate, which meant that he couldn't communicate with anyone through e-mail.

"We had made a one-year contract with the guy that we couldn't get out of and ended up spending way too much time talking about how to get rid of him without losing our asses and not enough time thinking about how to sell our products. I mean, we were actually considering whether or not it would be better to get rid of him and still pay him the thousands of dollars that he was entitled to by contract." Concludes Brandagee: "My one word of advice about all this is that if you have any hesitations about someone's character—who they are, where they're going—just don't even think about hiring them. You're wasting your time. We thought we needed to hire someone quickly, and that was producing a lot of anxiety itself. But we would have been much better off waiting another two months until we found someone who we were absolutely certain about."

So how can you be sure that you've got the right person before you actually bring them into your fold? "It's sort of akin to film-making, where casting is absolutely everything," notes Harry Gottlieb, the founder of Jellyvision, a CD-ROM development company. "If you're wrong for a particular part, it just doesn't matter how good an actor you may be. It's true with your friends, it's true with your significant others, and it's certainly true with your staff. So we put people through tests, especially the creative candidates. It's an audition process, where they write questions and develop content for our games for a couple months before we make up our minds. This is a hard company to get hired at. I'm not sure I could get hired here."

At Bliss, job candidates are put through similar paces, especially the ones that involve the most face-to-face contact. "The first thing people have to do before they can be hired here is to come in and give me a facial," says owner Marcia Kilgore, whose pores are squeaky clean. "I want to see how their hands are, what their their technique is, just to make sure they're normal. There are a lot of wacked-out people in the world, so if you're going to have employees working on people's faces, you want to try and make sure they're not one family short of a picnic."

If you've seen your candidate's handiwork elsewhere in the industry, that too is usually a good sign that they could work similar magic for you. "There was one big wine retailer in Atlanta that I was having trouble connecting with," says Vendemmia's Todd Alexander. "I guess I just hadn't been able to give them the attention they wanted right away because I was so busy doing other things. There was a woman who worked for a competitor who had a good relationship with them, and we happened to meet at a wine tasting. I made her an offer, she joined up, and we had the account soon after that."

One more caveat on the subject of hiring. Many young entrepreneurs fall into the trap of thinking that the economic power their mini enterprise wields will be enough to single-handedly pull all sorts of previously unemployable people out of poverty. Try to remember, however, that it will be enough of a miracle if your business works, and the taxes you'll pay will support plenty of government employment programs. In other words, you don't have to hire every person with a spotty job history who knocks on your door.

"You take it for granted that everyone knows what it means to work and that they all had a job after school when they were growing up," says Little Earth's Ava DeMarco. "But a lot of people have never worked and have parents who never worked. The idea that you have to set an alarm clock in the morning, that it's important to come in on time, that you should call in when you're sick—these ideas were totally new to some people." While Little Earth has had some success bringing these sorts of people around, you should seriously consider whether you have the time and energy to teach people these basic skills. "I wanted to give people a chance," says Dave Hirschkop of Dave's Gourmet, who hired one person with a drug problem and two who were on parole. "But most of the time, that sort of thing backfires on you. The people with checkered pasts that I hired usually haven't worked out over the long haul."

NO, THEY WON'T WORK FOR FREE

Handing out the job offers is only half the hiring equation, for no one will be prepared to make a commitment until they know what you're going to pay them. Even if you've got a big pile of venture capital money, neither you nor the people who gave it to you are going to want to see it spent on lofty salaries. The good thing about this is that most smart people who are considering working for a start-up understand that their payoff won't come in the first year. In fact, it may never come at all. Many people who seek out such jobs are looking for job satisfaction as much as anything else—the sort of opportunity where they'll be able to have a say in how things are run and see their stamp on the company. Sure, your employees will be psyched if you go public in five years and they all get rich with stock options, but most of them know it's a longshot. If it appears that they don't understand this, make sure you help them deal with reality before they come to work for you.

That said, you still have to pay your workers a living wage from day one. It's also smart to make some sort of tangible promise to prove that there's a financial upside for them if the company succeeds. The temptation may be to start handing out ownership of your company in 2 percent chunks, since it isn't worth that much in the beginning. Or you might be considering giving employees stock in your company, which could be sold back to you if they leave or cashed out if your company ever sells shares to the public.

In fact, many people who go to work for start-ups these days understand that they should have some sort of skin in the game, though their expectations are sometimes just a bit too lofty. "Some people just don't understand what's reasonable, like the junior employees who show up wanting 10 percent of the company because some friend told them that's what they should be asking for," says Career Central's Jeffrey Hyman. "So it's important to sit down and educate people about how potentially valuable even a small chunk of equity can be."

Before you give away anything, sit down with someone smart who can walk you through the numbers and the mechanics of it all. You don't need to hire a full-time human resources guru, as there are lots of lawyers and reasonably priced consultants out there who have helped hundreds of people just like you get through this maze. It's worth spending the money on good advice early on. That way, you avoid getting into a situation later where your company is worth $10 million but you end up penniless.

One way to avoid giving half your company away is to barter off the things you make or do in return for free labor. At Upper Limits, the upfront work necessary to turn the grain silos into climbing space was enormous. Chris and Pam Schmick couldn't do it all themselves, but they couldn't afford a crew of welders and demolition men either, since their business wasn't generating any income yet. Their solution? Bring in their friends to help haul away the several tons of steel and rotted soybeans that lined the silos and pay them in pizza and free climbing time. "We kept track of the number of hours people spent helping us," says Chris. "Some of them got lifetime memberships."

At Wet Feet Press, the owners couldn't quite afford to pay market rates to their employees, but they gave out bonuses. "We have an ongoing discussion about giving out stock options, but we wanted to find a way to give people a quicker return on their investment in going to work for us," says cofounder Gary Alpert. "So we decided to give out bonuses on an individual basis based on specific deliverables, like if a writer completed a certain number of insider company reports per month. A bonus plan communicates up front the need for people to perform at a certain level, and then it gives them something extra when they do."

But how are you supposed to know what sort of salary to give people in different jobs in the first place? This is another area where it's helpful to seek out the advice of people who have done this before. Most cities and states have membership organizations of small business owners who meet often to give each other advice. There are some national groups that do similar work as well (see the Resource Section for details). You can also ask your new employees what they made at their old jobs and try to put together a package of salary plus options or a potential bonus that comes close to meeting or beating what they used to earn.

One issue that you may face right away is whether to pay people an annual salary or simply pay them by the hour. For a long time, the great management minds in corporate America simply made this decision according to the color of one's collar. Service workers, laborers, and other blue-collar workers earned an hourly wage, while people who sat behind desks earned a salary. Robert Stephens fell into this trap when he started Geek Squad, but he changed his mind about the same time he stopped charging his customers by the hour. "I figured my employees would never come in again once I got rid of the time cards, but I was wrong," he says. "People aren't computers. I may be good at programming computers, but you can't program people. They don't want to be treated that way. Sure I'd rather have them leave for lunch, know that that's their lunch hour, and be sure they'll be back in 60 minutes." But he also knows that by ditching the time clock and displaying some faith in his employees' desire to do good work, he sent an incredibly positive message to them all. Plus, he saves a lot of money on bookkeeping.

Once you've figured the whole salary thing out, there's another matter: benefits. Most small companies simply don't bother with it, figuring that's one of the things that you just can't offer until the enterprise is bigger and profitable. It's even easier for young entrepreneurs to justify this sort of thinking since they and many of their workers are young enough to not need a doctor very often. If you do need urgent care, you can always go to the doctor, pay the full fee, and charge it on a credit card if you don't have the cash to pay the bill right away. You can also buy a relatively cheap policy to cover yourself in case a major catastrophe strikes.

With health coverage becoming an increasingly valued benefit in companies of all sizes, it probably shouldn't come as any big surprise that the few entrepreneurs who offer insurance consider it crucial to their success, since it makes them heroes with their employees. Take John Chuang at MacTemps. Not only does he offer insurance, but he does it in an industry where most of the workers are part-time and don't work for one company for very long. "When Clinton started talking about the health care system, I realized that our industry was part of the problem," he says. "We take our company's role in society pretty seriously, so we took a harder look at it to see if we could fix it.

"What we figured was that we could probably make money by offering health insurance because it would help us attract and retain the best people. So without a lot of study or analysis, we started looking for insurance companies who would help us. It took a while, because none of them were interested in insuring temporary workers at that time, but we were persistent and rammed our way through the bureaucracy. When that worked, we started offering a 401k plan too." If you needed to temp for a while, where would you want to work?

YOU WON'T WORK FOR FREE EITHER (WELL . . .)

You're not a temp of course—you're the boss. The big kahuna. The chairman of the board. So how much are you going to pay yourself, bigshot? The temptation is to pad your bank account to make it look like the captain of industry that you are, or at least the one you'd like to become. If you're smart, however, you'll let the parenting instinct overwhelm any delusions of grandeur you may have. Your business, after all, is your baby, and no baby grows up to be big and strong without a fair bit of investment at the grocery store. Money is the food that allows businesses to grow, so if you use it to line your bank account, there's a good chance you'll stunt the growth of your start-up.

You should probably also think a bit about how it will look to your employees if you've asked them to sacrifice without doing so yourself. "We're making a lot less than we were earning even before business school, let alone what we could be making now working for a large company," notes Wet Feet Press's Gary Alpert. "But we don't need money to buy suits. And we don't have time to take expensive vacations. And because we can't afford to pay market wages, people need to be willing to make a sacrifice to come work for us because they believe in what we're trying to do. We ought to set that example ourselves, so our salaries are among the lowest in the company."

Before Chris and Pam Schmick opened their Bloomington, Illinois, rock climbing gym, Upper Limits, to the public, they had been living in the town of Peru, 60 miles away. While Chris spent many months trying to whip the abandoned grain silos into shape, Pam stayed in Peru running a small health club. "I just slept in the office next to the silos so we didn't have to use money from our bank loans to pay two rents," Chris says. "Then when we opened up, we paid ourselves $9 an hour, just like everyone else who worked here. We plan on having our loans paid off in about four years, so there are no Ferraris parked outside yet."

Indeed, the truly austere consider their clunker cars a badge of honor. When John Chuang was profiled in *Forbes,* he posed for the photograph with his ten-year-old Toyota. His thinking on the whole subject, however, is much more advanced than simply making a statement with his choice of vehicles. "For the first five years or so, I paid myself about $30,000 annually," he says. "Now if I feel like I've done a good job I'll pay myself a little more. Last year, I didn't feel like I did so well, so I paid myself less. But whatever my salary is is not really the point. That's not where my net worth is, because that's all tied up in the company. So ultimately I'm getting paid well if the company does well. The salary itself doesn't really matter."

Just be careful not to overdo it. While it's important to build your business before you build your bank account, when you're practically starving, all that equity you've got doesn't do you a hell of a lot of good. "When we first got started, I had some savings to live on and a 401(k) account from working at *Sports Illustrated,"* says Julia Stern of Malia Mills. "So when it came time to make choices about whether to pay the fabric people or take money for a salary, it always made more sense to pay our suppliers. But you yourself have to be a priority from the get go. When you can't pay rent and the credit card people are calling to yell at you and the cable company is coming to disconnect your service for nonpayment, it distracts you from the business."

Once you've determined whom you want working for you and how much everyone is going to be paid, you actually have to tell them what to do. Managing your employees is difficult under the best of circumstances, as a brief glance at the miles of management books on the shelves of your local bookstore will demonstrate. In a start-up, where the pressure can be overwhelming and everything happens really fast, it's even tougher. Young entrepreneurs have it particularly tough. You may not have ever had a job before you started your company, so you may never have experienced management from the perspective of the managed. But even if you do have some experience in the working world, this will probably be the first time you've been solely responsible for things like making sure people's paychecks don't bounce so they can pay their rent.

IS THIS WHAT FRIENDS ARE FOR?

When it comes time to start giving orders, the most difficult challenges will probably come from dealing with two distinct sets of workers. The first are your friends. If you're like most young entrepreneurs, you'll want to make your first hires people whom you have the utmost trust in. Who better than your friends, right? Well, it may not be quite so simple once they're actually working for you and the power balance of your relationship has been significantly altered. "The one friend we hired ended up leaving, and when we wanted him to come back he said he didn't think it was a good idea for him to be working for friends," says Taste of Nature's Scott Samet. "In retrospect, I think it was more difficult for him than it was for us." Whether it's envy or simply wanting to keep friends rather than having them become your bosses, it's very difficult to be in the employees' shoes in these sorts of situations.

Then again, some of your friends may just view you and your business as a free ride. After all, you're their buddy, so there's no reason they have to work hard to impress you, right? "The same people who worked hard to help us get the place built were the ones who didn't feel like they had to work late once it was open," says Upper Limits's Chris Schmick. "We did owe them in a way, so we felt obligated to hire the ones who wanted jobs. But thank God most of them eventually took off, because the people who replaced them who aren't friends with us work a lot harder than they did. Now all those original people can just be our friends instead of our employees."

At least the Schmicks have managed to remain friendly with the people who slacked off on them. The real danger in having your friends as employees is that if things get screwed up at work, the friendship is likely to blow up as well. Obviously, the closer you are to someone, the more seriously you should consider the possibility that this might happen to you. "At one point I did hire one of my closest friends," says Dave Hirschkop. "I'm not very well organized, so I hired him to be the detail person, to keep track of the numbers and things like that. But he let things slide the same way I did, even though his job was not to let them slide. We parted ways, and it was a poor way to part. I almost never speak to him anymore."

That's not to say that you absolutely can't make it work. If you're going to try to pull it off, you need to be crystal clear with your friends from the beginning about what you expect of them. "The essential problem with these sorts of things is that you don't do the professional thing and hash out responsibilities because you were friends first, so you don't think you need to spell things out," says Tom Gardner of the Motley Fool. "You can't compromise yourself like that. You have to have contracts. They don't need to be high level and formal, but it should state exactly what this person's going to be doing for you."

Adds John Chuang, who has worked with a number of friends at MacTemps: "I just try to be very objective and open. You have to separate the personal feelings you have for them as friends and focus on their job performance—the accomplishments and achievements they've had and not mushy intangible things. To say someone is a poor leader isn't helpful. If they're head of the New York region and people are quitting and sales are down, then you have something more concrete to talk about."

HANDLING THE GRAYBEARDS

At first you might hire only friends and peers, so managing people your own age will be the only challenge you encounter. Eventually, however, you're going to have to give orders and instructions to people who are older than you are, whether they're employees, outside accountants, or vendors. This is the second group that will pose some tough managerial challenges. How do you get them to take you seriously and not treat you like a stupid kid who doesn't know what you're talking about? "One reason they respect our authority—and this has basically no merit—is that we've had so much exposure in the media," says David Gardner of the Motley Fool, which has been featured on the cover of *Fortune,* among other places. "Some people come in feeling like we're larger than life, when in fact you're just an average guy who does a lot of radio interviews. So there's a little bit of an aura that comes with that that could be damaging if you relied on it as a manager."

So you've come home from your ego trip. Now what? "There are a lot of good management books out there that tell you to say, 'I don't know a lot,' " Gardner continues. "Or, 'I'm not sure but I'll go get that answer for you.' Or to constantly remind yourself that you're in a support position to everyone that you manage, that you're essentially their servant—'You tell me what you need, and I'll try and get those resources for you.' " If you vocalize this stuff often, not only will people think that you're just a regular person, they'll actually feel like they can contribute to the process of solving the problems that come up in every business every day. "Older people get frustrated with younger people when they don't listen," notes Dave Hirschkop, who has managed many older workers at Dave's Gourmet. "You can't think that you know better simply because you're the boss and the business was all your idea in the first place."

PLAYING SHRINK

Unfortunately, not everyone is worth listening to all the time. And even the good employees may not have as many brain cells bouncing around inside their heads as you do. "Some people just aren't as competent as we'd like," says Taste of Nature's Scott Samet. "Some people don't pick things up as fast as others. Other people don't pay attention to the details we want them to pay attention to. It's like you constantly have to take a step back in order to move three steps forward."

Then again, it may not be a question of smarts at all but one of ownership, for no matter how many stock options you give away, your employees will probably never feel like it's their company too. "The hardest thing is to remember that employees won't have the same drive you do," says Chris Schmick of Upper Limits. "I have to remind myself all the time that I can't just expect that people are going to want to work overtime whenever we need them."

"No one ever had to tell me to do things two or three times, so I started with a pretty laissez-faire approach," adds Todd Alexander of Vendemmia. "I figured if I gave people a general idea of how I wanted things done that they would pick up the ball and run with it. But I learned early on that that's not how it works. Everyone hears the horror stories about jackass bosses, but I've found that I have to be more and more of a jackass if I want certain kinds of results. I hate the fact that that's true, but I'd rather be an asshole for a day than a nice guy with no business."

"I'm still known as something of a tyrant around here," says Robert Stephens of Geek Squad, who managed to be a lot tougher a lot sooner than Todd Alexander. "It's obvious that I have a healthy ego, and I've always been afraid that I'd end up being a dick of a boss. But I'm also fair. I've worked hard to try to cultivate people instead of controlling them. They make jokes about me, and I allow them to. Listen to me, 'I allow them to!' But I think they respect the fact that I'm not going water skiing every Saturday, and when we win another Best of Twin Cities award, I think they know that at the end of every day I'm getting better and we're getting better."

Still, you can't simply assume that there's a direct connection between the accolades your company receives and the way your employees feel about working there. "When we were hiring all our friends, it was easy, because they'd known us forever and understood what we were trying to do," says David Gardner of the Motley Fool. "They were already brainwashed. They knew it was all just a game, that it was going to be fun. But when you hire people who aren't your friends, they don't know that at all, so there has to be a core mission outlined for everyone. Now when people come in, they get notebooks full of the history of the company and all sorts of information about how we try to do things." This is no ordinary employee handbook either. Check out a passage from "The Fool Rules!" The following comes from the section on equal opportunity, where companies generally deliver the boilerplate about how they would never discriminate against anyone: "It must be noted however that this policy does have one notable exception. It is our strict and earnest intention—and our past record confirms it—to hire exclusively from among the living. Please note, therefore, that we absolutely refuse to consider for employment persons dead, deceased or otherwise coffinated. Cadavers continue to have no place at Fool HQ."

Sound like a cool place to work? Coolness is a tough aura to create and maintain, but that hasn't stopped people from trying. "When you can barely afford to pay market rates, there have to be other reasons for people to come to work in the morning," explains Career Central's Jeffrey Hyman. "I'm not an especially cool person, so I arranged for our office manager to visit a bunch of companies that appeared in the feature *Fortune* does each year about cool technology companies, just to see what they do that makes them cool. Now she has a budget for that stuff—rafting trips, T-shirts, and that sort of thing."

Trying to appeal to people's emotions like this is tricky, and traditionalists will tell you that it really doesn't matter all that much. Most Harvard M.B.A.'s tend to make fun of the soft skills they pick up in their classes on organizational behavior, which is a fancy term for the study of how people in corporations like to lie and cheat and stab each other in the backs. John Chuang, however, has tried to put a lot of it to work at MacTemps. "It heightened my awareness of what I was saying and how my own nonverbal communication said things that I maybe didn't intend to say." He notes also how carefully people examine the boss's behavior for clues about what they really think about you and your work. "I also started to pay more attention to what other people's actions said, things like where people sat during meetings, who was sitting near whom, and what that all really meant in terms of the way the group was interacting. We had someone who came in as a part of a merger, and when he first started coming to meetings, he would sit at the end of the table, often with several seats between him and everyone else. It didn't take much to hypothesize that he felt isolated from all of us, so we've begun taking more steps to make sure he feels welcome."

Sometimes, signs of trouble won't be quite so subtle. "The worst part about managing is when there is tension between individual employees and we have to play babysitter," says Taste of Nature's Scott Samet. "I want to sell. I want to sit here on the phone with my customers and drive our business forward. I do not want to sit there and make peace between Person A and Person B because somebody is being mean to somebody else."

Though it's a huge pain in the ass, Samet and Chu know that if they don't referee these disputes, no one else will. The key is to defuse such situations quickly. "This has been one of my main problems," notes CDNow's Jason Olim. "You have to deal with personnel problems quickly and openly, or else everyone ends up unhappy, including innocent bystanders. Unhappy staff members can make others unhappy very quickly."

HOW TO FIRE PEOPLE AND STILL SLEEP AT NIGHT

Unfortunately, making everyone happy again can sometimes mean getting rid of the people who are causing the problems. Almost everyone with any managerial experience agrees that firing someone is the hardest thing they've ever had to do. One way to make it a little easier is to remind yourself that you're not a greedy slave driver who's decided to decapitate the workers who aren't keeping up. "It's unfair for the other employees who are working so hard to stand by and feel good about what they're doing when someone else isn't pulling their weight," says Kate Spade. "If you're not a good enough manager to have the strength to say good-bye to someone who can't keep up like that, then you're creating a little bit of a cancer in your company."

It may not be so difficult to let someone go if they seem to be making clear efforts to sabotage your success. Dave Kapell ran up against this problem at Magnetic Poetry, and he said it was surprisingly easy to say good-bye once it was clear that one of his employees simply didn't want to do what she was supposed to be doing. "I think I've become a lot more pragmatic, maybe even a little bit ruthless," he says. "I had told this woman that there were a lot of opportunities for advancement at our company, but I made it clear that at that moment, all I needed was help in customer service. But immediately, right after she started, she wanted to take accounting classes because her dream was to become the controller. She started to meddle in the accounting department, and it got to the point where she was actually digging into people's drawers, trying to figure out what other people were up to. She was calling people at home, trying to become their friends. It got to the point where I thought we might be liable for a harassment suit, and she got fired. It was the first time we felt we had to fire someone."

Firing gets more difficult when you have to let someone go only because they lack the aptitude necessary to do their work. It may help you feel better if you can think of a few nice things to say when you let people go and don't send them packing without some sort of safety net. "The first employee I had to fire was a super-nice guy, but he wasn't the brightest bulb. It took him a long time to ring up sales at the cash register, and he couldn't alphabetize the CDs properly," Altitunes's Amy Nye Wolf recalls. "You can't let it get to your emotions, though. I didn't make excuses. I just told him that I thought that another company could make better use of his skills. He was only a cashier, but I gave him a very generous severance package and he actually thanked me for having given him the opportunity."

Things really bottom out, however, when you have to let people go because you screwed up and hired more people than you actually needed. "Laying those people off was the single most difficult thing we've had to do so far," says Wet Feet Press's Gary Alpert. "We just weren't getting enough return on our investment in salary with the eight people we had. For instance, we thought it made sense to produce as many reports as we could, but once you have them, you have to keep them updated. And some of them weren't selling that many copies, so it wasn't worth it to have so many full-time people working on all those reports. We let them go at the same time we were moving into nice new offices too, but fortunately they were able to understand that we really were actually saving some money by moving in here and subleasing some of the space."

MESSING UP (AND WHY IT'S SOMETIMES WORTHWHILE)

At least Alpert and his partner had the good sense to realize that they had messed up and tried to do something to fix it. Whether it's overhiring, selling the wrong products, or not moving into new markets fast enough, you're bound to make a long list of strategic blunders in your first few years in business. There is no shame in this. "Failure is part of the process," says CDNow's Jason Olim. "Mistakes are the bricks with which you build businesses." It may sound like he's reading out of a textbook of management clichés. But by the 27th time you've screwed something up really badly (and it will happen that many times, no matter how successful you are), you'll need to repeat Olim's mantra to yourself as well.

So how can you recognize your mistakes before they become

big enough to really hurt your business? First, remember that the people best able to notice what a mess you're making are the ones who know your work best: your employees. So whether it's your strategy or simply your leadership that they're questioning, show some humility and create an atmosphere where they feel like you'll hear them out.

"We had established this whole ethic early on of accepting criticism graciously," says Harry Gottlieb whose company, Jellyvision, creates CD-ROM games. "But we had a retreat in the summer of 1996 to talk about how things were working, and I just got the shit beaten out of me. Most problems in the company came back to me: There was no money because we didn't have any venture capital, and the hours were too long. I always thought that if the products turned out great, everyone would be happy, but if a company exists for more than a certain period of time, people begin to think about their careers and not just the next great product.

"So the whole thing was excruciating for me. I was so wound up, because I thought that I was working for them as much as they were working for me, so my first response was 'Those ungrateful shits!' But intellectually I knew I had to take it in and I couldn't be defensive. So I did a lot of listening, and the year after that I had to go from being Washington leading the Revolution, trying to get the first big products out, to trying to govern the administration once we'd won. I can't believe Washington could do that. I can't believe anyone could do that. It takes two very different personalities to do those things, and I knew I had to change mine from one to the other or the company wouldn't survive."

If your employees aren't bold enough to dress you down the

way Gottlieb's did, you can be sure that the market will. "In 1990, we created a company called ThinkTemps, figuring that since MacTemps had been successful until that point, there was no reason why we couldn't compete in the market for general temporary help," recalls John Chuang, who chuckles about the experience now, takes a deep breath, and lets fly. "We started it at the wrong time, because the recession had just hit. We did it in the wrong place, because we had the offices set up in retail storefronts to attract people off the street, but that sort of space is incredibly expensive. We were using the wrong customer list—the one from MacTemps—for marketing. After all, those people used Macs, so if they needed temps they wouldn't get them from some general temp company. We tested candidates wrong. We gave them brain-teaser tests, but who cares if you know how to do that stuff? What we needed to know was if these people had basic math skills. So that led us to hiring the wrong kind of temps." At least Chuang had the good sense to know what a disaster he had brewed, and ThinkTemps was disbanded within five months.

At Clementine, it took about twice as much time for Elizabeth Burke and Abby Messitte to realize that their strategy needed tweaking. "We thought we could appeal to more people by selling a lot of $500 pieces, but at the rate we're going, we're just barely breaking even," says Elizabeth Burke. What they've found is that the younger customers they were aiming at think just as hard about buying a $500 print as someone twice their age would about purchasing one that costs ten times more. So if the two of them can put the same amount of effort in but earn ten times more profit, it makes sense to sell some more expensive work at least some of the time.

"Now that people know our reputation for showing interesting work and being more customer friendly than the other galleries, I think it will be all right to have a couple shows each year where we sell pieces that are more expensive," Burke says. "We have to do that if we're going to reach any kind of financial comfort level."

Other times, your strategic errors will reveal themselves only over time, and they'll often be fairly subtle. After Tom Baron and Juno Yoon were successful with their Mad Mex restaurant in Pittsburgh, they realized that there were all sorts of other cuisines that Pittsburgh was missing out on. So they opened a Caribbean spot, a pan-Asian restaurant, and a place serving American comfort food, among others.

When the two partners sat back and looked at the mini empire they had developed and thought hard about what their goals were, however, they realized that the two weren't quite compatible. "We want to grow a large national restaurant company, and to do that you have to focus on a concept," Baron explains. "What we should have done is stopped and focused on Mad Mex, which is our biggest money maker, and expanded that. But we let our egos get in the way. We knew that the town needed new things, and they were loving everything we gave them, so we figured we should just keep on going. But now we're in a position where we've created this monster, where it's really a pain in the ass to take care of all these individual concepts. We're in a situation now where if we open any new restaurants, we'll start to steal customers from our other spots."

Now, the pair are raising money to take Mad Mex to other underserved metropolitan areas and large college towns, something they think they should have done at least a year or two sooner. It's not the only management mistake the two partners have made, and every time they screwed up they've been smart enough to admit it to themselves quickly and fix the problem. Good managers don't always get it right the first time, but they do get it right eventually.

CHAPTER 9

IN SEARCH OF GURUS

How to Know When to Call in the Adults

The start-up phase is no time for stoicism.

No matter how many smart employees you hire, no matter how experienced your partners are, there will be many moments when you will be totally stumped. What was Dave Kapell supposed to do when six competitors showed up peddling knockoff poetry kits? What was John Chuang supposed to say to the dozens of bankers who have wanted to take MacTemps public? This sort of confusion is bound to strike any entrepreneur starting a business for the first time, but for young entrepreneurs who don't have much work experience to draw on, it's especially likely to happen.

HELP FROM THE HOME FRONT

Given all the challenges you're facing down, it's important not to try to figure everything out for yourself. "The first lesson in being smart is realizing that you're not," says Jason Olim of CDNow. "I knew at the outset that I didn't know what I was doing. I had no ego. And I asked everyone I knew for help, for everything from legal advice to office furniture. It's easy to make a nuisance of yourself if you take it too far, and some people will scoff at you as if you're just another dumb kid starting a business, which I was. But even more people thought that it was great that I was trying to start a company, and they gave me all sorts of help."

Where's the best place to start? Since Olim was living at home when he started CDNow, he figured the best place to start was with his parents and their friends. "My folks had a friend who was a lawyer in a small firm," he recalls. "They charged us a $250 per month retainer, which was worth about an hour of their time. We were taking up more like $5,000 of their time, but they loved it. They had never been involved in anything like this before, so for them it was a neat diversion."

Indeed, don't underestimate the enthusiasm you may inspire in the minds of people who are twice your age. Many of them are living comparatively stable lives on the middle rungs of the corporate ladder, perhaps wishing that they had had the courage 10 or 20 years ago to do what you're doing. They'll only be too glad to experience it vicariously, as Olim's family friend did. Todd Alexander's brother, who is a financial planner, helps him keep Vendemmia's numbers in shape. Amy Nye Wolf's father plays devil's advocate to poke her plans full of holes when he feels like she needs that. The list goes on and on.

As long as you're exploiting every last connection that your parents have, don't forget that they, like Wolf's father, may also have some business experience that could be helpful. It's probably been a while since you took anything your parents said very seriously, but it's funny how the older you get, the smarter they seem to become. "There were all these years when I was a teenager when my mother didn't seem to know anything," says Pam Schmick of Upper Limits, the rock-climbing gym in central Illinois. "Now, all of the sudden, she's starting to make sense again."

People who have had entrepreneurial success themselves are another great resource. They know exactly what it's like to be in your shoes and remember all the older people who helped them out when they were young and clueless. Now it's payback time. Tom First of Nantucket Nectars recalls one of his parents' friends, the guy who had founded Stride-Rite shoes. "He had just given up day-to-day management to go to law school, and he was insistent that if we ever needed legal help, we should call him. Then he called us like five times to see how things were going early on. Even when the product we were producing wasn't that good, he kept reminding us that we were never going to have a chance to do something like this again."

BUSINESS SCHOOL WISDOM WITHOUT THE M.B.A.

Not everyone has parents with a lot of business smarts or connections to people who do. If you don't have personal connections, try your local business school, which can be a terrific resource. While John Chuang got a lot of mileage for MacTemps by simply enrolling as a full-time M.B.A., you don't have to spend a cent of tuition dollars to exploit the big brains there for your own good. "Have you ever seen the *Three's Company* episode where Jack is taking the guitar lessons and the next day he's giving the lesson to somebody else?" asks CDNow's Jason Olim. "Well I had a friend in business school who did the same thing for me. I would call him up and tell him about some human resources problem we were having, and he'd say, 'Funny you should mention that, because I just had a class about that last week.' He taught me how to read a financial model and a bunch of other stuff too. He's really had a big impact on this business."

Business schools are also great sources of free or cheap labor, as they all have small business development centers or entrepreneur clubs teeming with students who want to get some experience putting their classroom knowledge to work. "They taught me a lot," says Olim, who put some M.B.A. students to work one summer polishing his books. "They built our first revenue and cost projection model, which was real yeoman's work. They were really smart, and we had three of them there for free all summer."

One caveat here: these students aren't that much more experienced than you are, so you may be better off putting them to work on technical projects like the one Olim's students were engaged in. Once they were done with the model, the students (mistakenly) determined that Olim ought to shut down and give up before Tower Records came online and ran him out of business. Two years after Tower showed up online, the company was still doing a fraction of CDNow's business.

If you're not interested in putting students to work, it's possible to go straight to the source and get free advice from the professors themselves. There's a boom in demand right now for business schools to teach more specialized entrepreneurship classes and to integrate more case studies of small businesses into the overall curriculum. This is something that most schools ignored until the mid-1990s, and they still don't have a good idea of how to integrate it into their classrooms. One method they're testing, however, is to simply bring entrepreneurs in as guest speakers. If you offer yourself up, you stand a good chance of developing a relationship with professors you can turn to later on.

"More than anything I've read or studied to improve our business, I probably learned the most from the guest lectures we've done at Harvard and Babson," says Nantucket Nectars's Tom Scott, noting that the exchange between students and professors who attend is always incredibly thought provoking. "There's one professor at Harvard who knows our business really well. They decided to write a case study on us, so we've met with him a bunch of times and he's been really helpful."

Instead of dropping $50,000 on an M.B.A., you might also pick and choose from the extensive night school curriculum offered by business schools. Think about it this way: tuition for one of these classes costs maybe $500, but if you were to try to hire the professor as a consultant, that money would maybe buy you a couple hours of his time. "You are nuts if you don't take some of these classes," says Little Earth's Rob Brandagee. Not only did he learn a lot, but one of his professors also ran the university's small business development center. She was well connected with city officials and put Brandagee and his partner in touch with people who got the company tax breaks because of their location in a rundown section of Pittsburgh.

EVEN THE GOVERNMENT CAN HELP

If there isn't a good business school nearby, or you've already tapped it for all it's worth, a number of other resources are available all over the country. The Service Corps of Retired Executives, or SCORE, is an offshoot of the U.S. Small Business Administration, and it's one of the few government programs that actually does its job efficiently. Each local chapter is made up of volunteer retirees from the community who are former executives from large companies or who ran businesses themselves. When you call, it's sort of the luck of the draw whom you end up with, but if you're persistent you can find a good match. "At first, we got hooked up with this lame guy who sort of treated us like cute little girls with an art store," recalls Abby Messitte of Clementine. "But SCORE also led us to a small business counselor at Baruch College who was enormously helpful. He gave us homework and got us thinking about a number of issues that we hadn't considered."

CHASE DOWN YOUR IDOLS

Sometimes, the very people who have succeeded in the industry that you want to play in yourself will be willing to talk to you. You would think that they wouldn't want to assist a potential competitor, but that's not always the case. "I made all these cold calls that I totally had to psyche myself up for to people who owned galleries," says Elizabeth Burke, Messitte's partner at Clementine. "I was contacting gallery owners and other people who were way out of my league. I was a nobody to them, but because I was a nobody, they didn't see me as a threat. You would think these people are totally inaccessible, but then you realize that they aren't and that you can do this. Everyone was really accommodating, and it was actually kind of fun." Indeed, most people in these sorts of positions remember what it was like to be in your shoes just starting out, and if they have any decency at all they'll make at least some attempt to throw the rope back for you.

Malia Mills had a similar experience when she sought help from an executive at DKNY, a large New York City designer. "Looking back now, my drawing skills were almost laughable," she says. "But she sat down with me and told me what she would be looking for if they were adding a swimwear line, which ideas of mine she thought were good, and how she would take them further. This was a total stranger talking to someone who might be competition one day, but she was very encouraging. She made me feel like I kind of had a talent for this."

Remember, it's important to have a targeted list of ideas or problems you want to discuss with people like this; otherwise, you run the risk of wasting their time. Now that Mills is on the other side of the desk, she understands this well. "A lot of people show up here who are very curious about how to break into this business, but they don't know how to ask the right questions," she says. "They're so wildly interested that they haven't focused on anything, and that wastes their time and ours. Is it the craft with their hands, or the conception with their brain, or dresses, or men's, or children's, or retail or wholesale? We all go through that initial confusion, but you have to narrow it down some before people can help you make it happen."

Still, you may not want to seem utterly smooth, either, lest the people you're seeking out really do perceive you as a threat. Take it from Alex Kramer, a private investigator as well as a young entrepreneur, who says that not looking the part has been one key to her success. "A woman has the ability to get a lot of information because she is less intimidating than a man," she explains. "People are more willing to talk to you. I also never dress up, because when I do, people at courthouses and other places will think that I'm a lawyer, and nobody likes lawyers. You don't want to look like a bike courier either, but you get the idea."

John Chuang was the first person to start a temporary agency specializing in people skilled on the Macintosh computer, so there wasn't anyone who came before him that fit his aspirations exactly. So while he did steal some ideas from a temp agency he had worked for after high school, he looked to his merchant neighbors in Harvard Square for much of his inspiration. "We bothered all our neighbors," he says. "You just look for ideas wherever you can find them. We'd run things by them, see what they were doing and how it was working."

SELF-HELP GROUPS

Alex Kramer has a whole circle of friends who are small business owners, and she calls on them regularly for advice. "I guess it's sort of my support group," she says. "There's a woman who has her own landscaping business, and I talk to her about how she hires short-term employees. There's one who has a law firm and another with a clothing store. The big joke is, since we're not in the corporate world anymore, there aren't any company-sponsored holiday parties or Christmas bonuses. So we figure we should go out on a certain night and just pass our checks to the left so someone else can pay for us."

There are more formal ways to network like this too. National organizations that aim to help young entrepreneurs run their businesses better are listed in the Resource Section. For every business, no matter how obscure, there's also bound to be a trade organization made up of people who do similar things. It's worth joining and going to the annual conventions if there are any, since they tend to be a hotbed of good ideas. "There's an amazing camaraderie there," Kramer says of her communication with other investigators. "People are willing to exchange information, since we're all part of the information business. Some of them have even handed work off to me when I've been slow and they've been overwhelmed." See the Resource Section for more on how to find groups like these.

THE CUSTOMER IS ALWAYS RIGHT

Your customers generally have a pretty good idea of whether you're doing a good job, so ask them for advice too. "For the first several months, every time we had someone on the phone we'd ask them how they heard about us, whether they'd seen any of our products, and what they thought about them," says Wet Feet Press's Gary Alpert. "We also started asking them the same questions on our Web site. One thing they told us a lot was that they were having trouble finding prices. We tracked how they were navigating the site, what search terms they were using to find things, and refined the site accordingly. It was at that point that our sales online started growing exponentially from month to month. The correlation was totally direct between us asking for feedback and the sales bumping up to a whole new level."

SEND IN THE PROS

Alpert and his partner have a pretty good sense of how good their products are now, but they're less convinced that they have a handle on their own overall performance as managers and owners. "The hardest part about all this is that there's no one here to evaluate our work," he says. "No one tells us how we're doing. We do it a little bit with each other, but we're also way too understanding of all the constraints we both face. In our past jobs, we've always had a ton of feedback, and it's hard to not have that anymore." Your investors—if you have any—are likely to have pretty strong feelings about what you're doing well and what could be improved, so it's smart to turn to them for regular feedback.

A lot of the advice that Alpert and others crave is for sale if you're willing to pay for it. Though you generally don't read much about it in the business press, there's a whole industry of executive coaches and other consultants out there available to pick over you and your company in fine detail. "He's what I refer to as our gray matter," says Dave Kapell of Magnetic Poetry. "He's an older guy who worked for Tonka Toys for many years, and I discovered that he had a lot of good advice to offer once I got the wax out of my ears."

Kapell used his consultant's services somewhat sparingly, for it cost him $50 an hour to have the guy around. Robert Stephens has a similar setup. "He's a paid mentor, sort of like Mr. Miyagi from *The Karate Kid,*" he says. In fact, he found him so useful that he knew he wasn't going to be able to afford to pay him for long. "He normally costs $300 an hour, but I knew I needed him. I could tell that it would take me a lot longer to grow my company in the right way without the help of someone like him. So he told me that because he liked my company, he would just write me a check for whatever we decided 10 percent of my business was worth, and that way he would have a stake in it and a reason to help me out. It's sort of like a partnership, but I'm still the dictator. But I can call him for advice whenever I want, and I still listen to him before I do something impulsive. My employees can also talk to him if they feel like they can't come to me about something."

Most people seek out investors simply for their cash, not realizing that it's their advice that could ultimately make or break your business. Though Stephens didn't really need the money, he figured that this arrangement was the only way he could afford the help that he needed. This is not normally the way consultants discount their services, but since Stephens hadn't yet given up any equity the arrangement has served him well so far. After all, since his consultant has his own skin in the game, he has every incentive to give Stephens as much good advice as possible. Not a bad deal.

EPILOGUE

NOW WHAT?

So what do you want to be when you grow up?

This question is what began this whole discussion, and it's not a bad one on which to end it too. If you've decided to forget about starting a company and are going to stay in corporate America for a while longer, that's cool. It doesn't make you a coward. After all, big company life is fraught with as much risk these days as being an entrepreneur, for you could get fired at any time and should probably expect it to happen at some point in your career. Still, most of the big lumbering giants have changed their cultures enough by now to appreciate a young upstart in their midst who has some good ideas. So it's not impossible to take some of what you might have learned in these pages and put it to work in a larger enterprise.

But hopefully you've been inspired enough by what you've

read here to make a go of it yourself at some point soon. As Jeffrey Hyman of Career Central suggested, even if your business doesn't make it or if you sell out after a few years, you'll have built so many skills that you'll be immediately employable if you want to work for someone else. Chances are, however, that by then you'll have caught the entrepreneurial bug, and working for yourself will have become sort of like a drug. "Hey, if I don't like the way things work out for me here, I can go do something else," says Andrew Koven. "The same way I started two businesses, I can just go out and start a third." In fact, as this book was heading to the printer, he had sold Collegiate Sales and Marketing and was looking for yet another entrepreneurial opportunity.

The Serial Entrepreneur: Casting Off from Corporate America and Becoming an Upstart for Life. It would make a good title for another book, don't you think? Here's hoping that some of you will end up in its pages.

THE UPSTARTS AND THEIR START-UPS

Altitunes
Amy Nye Wolf

Bliss
Marcia Kilgore

Career Central for MBAs
Jeffrey Hyman and Lun Yuen

CDNow
Jason Olim

Clementine Gallery
Elizabeth Burke and Abby Messitte

Collegiate Sales and Marketing
Andrew Koven

Dave's Gourmet
Dave Hirschkop

Geek Squad
Robert Stephens

Guaranteed Resumes
Kevin Donlin

Jellyvision
Harry Gottlieb

Kate Spade
Kate Spade and Andy Spade

Alex Kramer, PI
Alex Kramer

Little Earth
Rob Brandagee and Ava DeMarco

MacTemps
John Chuang

Mad Mex
Tom Baron and Juno Yoon

Magnetic Poetry
Dave Kapell

Malia Mills
Malia Mills and Julia Stern

Motley Fool
David Gardner and Tom Gardner

Nantucket Nectars

Tom First and Tom Scott

Taste of Nature

Doug Chu and Scott Samet

Upper Limits

Chris and Pam Schmick

Vendemmia

Todd Alexander

Wet Feet Press

Gary Alpert and Steve Pollock

RESOURCE SECTION

Given that most of you will be trying to start a company while you're also full-time students or employees of somebody else, time is of the essence. You can't digest the entire library or visit every one of the thousands of Web sites aimed at entrepreneurs. So I've tried to winnow it down here to the best titles, people, and places for you to turn to.

GENERAL HELP

Books

Kiplinger's Working for Yourself, by Joseph Anthony. Kiplinger/Times Business.

This is an incredibly thorough look at all the issues you'll face when you consider starting your own company. It includes particularly helpful sections on figuring out whether you can afford to work for yourself, naming your company, and picking a partner, as well as chapters on franchising, multilevel marketing, and buying a business from someone else.

Going Indie, by Kathi Elster and Katherine Crowley. Kaplan/Simon & Schuster.

This book is a much cheaper version of one of those self-assessment bubble tests that professional career counselors and university placement offices will try to get you to take. You're better off with this book, which asks you plenty of searching questions and is particularly useful for people who want to start one-person businesses.

The E-Myth Revisited, by Michael Gerber. Harper Business.

Gerber begins with the premise that most small businesses don't work, meaning that, while they may not fail immediately, they still go down the tubes within three to five years of starting up. Why is this? Gerber thinks it has less to do with market forces than with the psychological make-up of individual entrepreneurs. If you're in the mood for some soul-searching, this one's a classic.

Why Entrepreneurs Fail, by James Halloran. McGraw Hill.

Halloran looks at a whole bunch of reasons why entrepreneurs fail, including location, bad leases, poor pricing decisions, living off your cash flow instead of your profits, inventory troubles, and expanding for the wrong reasons.

Anatomy of a Start-Up, edited by Elizabeth Longsworth.

This is a collection of columns from *Inc.* magazine, where they dissect one newish company and then put their case study to a panel of experts who give advice on what the company ought to do to survive. If you liked the profiles in *Upstart Start-Ups!,* you'll probably get a lot out of this book too.

Startup, by Jerry Kaplan. Penguin.

This is Kaplan's own tale of his attempts to start and grow a company called Go Corporation. While its main product, a hand-held computer operated with a pen instead of a keyboard, was a bit before its time, there's a lot to be learned from Kaplan's Silicon Valley saga.

How to Get Ideas, by Jack Foster. Berrett-Koehler.

Foster spent 35 years in the ad business searching for great ideas for print ads and commercials. While that's not quite the same thing as looking for business ideas, his techniques make a lot of sense (they've helped me a lot in coming up with story ideas for *Fortune).* While his approach sounds sort of cutesy—act more like a kid, have fun, don't be afraid—it's just the sort of fresh point of view that most baby boomers lack.

The Perfect Business Plan Made Simple,
by William Lasher. Doubleday.

Business Plans for Dummies,
by Paul Tiffany and Steven Peterson. IDG.

There are dozens of books in print on writing a business plan, but these are two of the best. The *Dummies* book is particularly comprehensive.

Teaming Up: The Small Business Guide to Collaborating with Others to Boost Your Earnings and Expand Your Horizons,
by Paul and Sarah Edwards. Tarcher/Putnam.

This is a good book for people who are still deciding whether they want a business partner, but it's also helpful for small companies that hope to latch onto bigger partners who might be able to help them boost sales. Before you sign any licensing agreements with a behomoth, check out this book for information on how to avoid being ripped off and how to know when a partnership has run its course.

Magazines

The biggest magazines for people trying to start their own business are *Entrepreneur, Inc.,* and *Success,* though if you hit any large bookstore, you're bound to find 10 or 15 more titles as well. The bigger business magazines can also be helpful. *Business Week* is a good roundup for people who don't have time to read the news in the *Wall Street Journal* (though I strongly urge anyone with even the slightest interest in business to read it daily). *Fortune* (my home) offers a lot of good management advice and excellent coverage of technology. *Fast Company,* the newest title in this group, is sort of a management magazine for the 21st century; it is aimed at a younger audience that plans to be in the game for a long time.

All these publications can be read more or less for free online, and some offer great resources on the Web that you can't get by reading the paper versions.

www.entrepreneurmag.com Here you get access to the main magazine, plus another title called *Business Start-Ups.* But the best thing about the site is the archive of lists that the magazine publishes: best franchises, 50 businesses to start now—that sort of thing. It's good for idea fishing. There's also a helpful feature that allows you to search for trade shows in your industry.

www.inc.com On this site, you get tips of the day, follow-ups on recent stories that have appeared in the magazine, plus *zinc,* an online zine for young entrepreneurs. *zinc* includes profiles of young entrepreneurs like the ones you've read in this book, plus links to other sites you might find helpful.

www.successmagazine.com This site is notable for something called the Source, which is a huge collection of links and resources. You could spend hours browsing this thing.

Web Sites

Before you hit the Web, keep in mind that all the major online services plus all the major search engines tend to have dedicated features for entrepreneurs. The advantages to looking at these things first is that they tend to be more well organized than the average Web site, plus they'll link you to sites that they've preselected as being particularly good. While the Web is constantly in flux, I'm reasonably sure that these sites will still exist by the time you pick this book up.

www.business.gov This is a site designed to get you answers to any questions you might have for the government when you're starting a business. Where do you go to get stamps when you're working 100 hours per week and don't have time to stand in line at the post office? Which I.R.S. forms must your employees fill out? This site also has an internal search engine that will help get you to the right spots.

www.sba.gov This is the official site of the U.S. Small Business Administration, and it has a number of nice features. For instance, with a few quick clicks you can point to your state on a map and get all the information you need about local and regional SBA offices and what services they offer. You'll also find a truly comprehensive tutorial on writing your business plan, a schedule of SBA training seminars near you, and a ton of information on all the agency's loan programs. (You can also call the SBA answer desk for even more information at 1-800-827-5722.)

www.smallbiz.suny.edu Despite the address, which makes it seem like this is an academic site, this is actually the best way for you to track down something called a Small Business Development Center (SBDC). These centers are sponsored by the SBA and are often located at a local university, where counselors will help you with your business plan, market research, and anything else you want to bounce off them. The partners at Clementine had a lot of success using this service, so it's worth a look if there's one near you. (You can reach the Association of Small Business Development Centers at 202-887-5599.)

www.score.org SCORE, which stands for the Service Corps of Retired Executives, offers the same kind of advice and support you'd get from an SBDC, except it's doled out by grizzled veterans who've been in the trenches themselves. Entrepreneurs who have used this service say it's kind of hit or miss; while you may not find many retirees who know much about Internet businesses, if you're planning on opening a retail store you may find someone who'll offer terrific advice. (The Web site can direct you to the SCORE branch nearest you, or you can call 1-800-634-0245.)

Membership Organizations

Young Entrepreneur's Network. 617-867-4690
(www.idye.com)

Included among this organization's services are a newsletter, a directory of other entrepreneurs, a consulting division, and a discount program to help you get good deals on office furniture and long-distance services.

Young Entrepreneur's Organization. 1-800-804-3688
(www.yeo.org)

A sort of higher-octane version of Young Entrepreneur's Network. The dues here are really steep (about $1,100 annually), but the company is really good, according to Andrew Koven of Collegiate Sales and Marketing.

National Association for the Self-Employed 1-800-232-6273.
(www.selfemployed.nase.org)

NASE is essentially a lobbying organization, and it works over members of Congress to ensure that tax laws and other government regulations don't penalize people who work for themselves. Occasionally, they even manage to negotiate a tax break or two, so it's an institution well worth supporting. Annual dues are about $75, which includes discounts on travel and insurance.

National Federation of Independent Businesses.
415-341-7441.

Similar to NASE, though NASE tends to have more members that run home-based businesses, while NFIB's membership consists of companies that are a little bit bigger. Dues range from about $100 to about $1,000, depending on the size of your company. While this is more expensive than NASE, NFIB maintains lobbying arms in all 50 states.

In search of a trade group for your particular industry? Most of them are listed in *The Encyclopedia of Associations,* which most libraries have. Just look up ice cream or handbags (or whatever) in the index, and it will point you to all the listings under that heading within its pages.

Steve Jobs

Yup, this is *the* Steve Jobs, founder of Apple Computer. At the time this book was being printed, he was in the middle of trying to save the company while also running his newest venture, Pixar. Of all that's been written about Steve Jobs and the founding of Apple, there's one little-known fact that's of real use to young entrepreneurs. When Apple was just starting out, Jobs brashly called Bill Hewlett, cofounder of Hewlett Packard, and asked for some advice. The two struck up a friendship, and ever since, Jobs has always made a point of taking calls from other upstarts to help them in the same way that Hewlett helped him. Give him a try at 510-236-4000, which is the main switchboard at Pixar.

MARKETING

Promoting Your Business with Free, or Almost Free, Publicity, by Donna Albrecht. Prentice Hall.

This a thorough, well-thought-out title. Sections include working together with other businesses and professional organizations to spread your good name, the importance of doing community service work, working with schools, pulling crazy stunts, contests, getting published, doing seminars, online publicity, and much more.

Entrepreneur's Successful Advertising for Small Businesses, by Conrad Berke. John Wiley.

This book starts by asking a perfectly good question—Who needs it?—and then follows up with another important one—Are you prepared for the onslaught of business if it actually works? There are also sections on budget planning and uses of alternative media.

MONEY

Books

Entrepreneur's Guide to Raising Money. John Wiley.

Entrepreneur magazine has put out a series of good books about all aspects of starting your own company, and this one is particularly well done. Chapters include an explanation of how the SBA can and can't help you, info on getting suppliers and others to extend you credit, and a treatise on bootstrapping for people who don't have success with any of the other financing methods. The book also includes a great resource section.

Borrowing to Build Your Business, by George M. Dawson. Upstart.

This book does a good job of putting you in the shoes of the banker who's been trained to think of every possible reason to turn down your loan application. There's also a helpful section letting you in on several questions bankers will always ask, and how to answer them.

How to Get a Business Loan Without Signing Your Life Away,
by Joseph R. Mancuso. Fireside.

There are helpful chapters here on business plans and SBA loans, but the best advice offered is on how you can avoid having to sign a personal guarantee, which is what banks try to stick you with so that they can take your house and all your belongings if your business fails.

Pratt's Guide to Venture Capital Sources.
Securities Data Publishing.

Just what it sounds like, a detailed list of most of the VCs in America. This should be in the reference section at most public libraries, which is the first place you should look for it, since it costs about $300.

The Venture Capital Handbook,
by David Gladstone. Prentice Hall.

Gladstone, who is a venture capitalist himself, offers a ton of detailed advice and some good laughs too. Sections include "VCs are Paranoid" and "Things You Never Say to a Venture Capitalist." Gladstone promises to review your own business plan himself if you send it to him in the mail and have used the format he lays out for you in his book.

A Basic Guide for Valuing a Company,
by Wilbur M. Hegge. John Wiley.

Eat your spinach. Sooner or later you're going to have to sit down and figure out how much your company is worth, whether it's at the beginning when you're wrangling with the venture capitalists or when someone calls out of the blue wanting to buy you out. This book is written in plain English, without a lot of financial mumbo jumbo, and it includes many helpful case studies.

Web Sites

www.ideacafe.com This site is a sort of all-purpose Web zine for budding entrepreneurs, and it's nicely written and pretty to look at. But the best parts about it are the extensive listings and links on financing your business.

www.financehub.com This site offers a VC seekers showcase—basically a listing service for companies in search of capital. There are also articles by a number of entrepreneurs who successfully navigated the VC maze, links to VC firms, and a bunch of information about banks and legal issues.

www.pw.com/vc This site is maintained by Price Waterhouse, the big international accounting and consulting firm. Each quarter, it does an extensive survey of venture capitalists to find out how much money they're lending, who's lending the most, what sort of companies they're giving it to, and what stage of growth those companies are in. This site is incredibly helpful if you're trying to get a handle on what's hot and where.

www.vfinance.com This site holds the Venture Capital Resource Library, which includes links to some of the most well-known VC firms in America. They also offer a free e-mail newsletter.

www.pricap.com This is a site for something called the Private Capital Clearinghouse, which helps put entrepreneurs together with angel investors. There's also a useful section called the Education Center, which offers useful ideas on business plans and general information on angel investing.

A WORD ABOUT GUERRILLAS

Jay Conrad Levinson is the ultimate upstart. He left a cushy career as an advertising executive to forge a path as an alterna-guru for entrepreneurs, and he's been amazingly successful. His books are about how you can be a thorn in your competitor's side and succeed mightily without breaking the bank. They're all published by Houghton Mifflin.

The Way of the Guerrilla
Guerrilla Marketing
Guerrilla Marketing Excellence
Guerrilla Marketing Attack
Guerrilla Marketing Weapons
Guerrilla Marketing for the Home-Based Business
Guerrilla Marketing Online
Guerrilla Financing
Guerrilla Selling
Guerrilla Advertising
Guerrilla Trade Show Selling

A FEW MORE BOOKS ABOUT YOUNG ENTREPRENEURS

If I thought these books were the last words on entrepreneurship, I wouldn't have written my own. Still, there's very little out there written specifically for people in our age group, and these books offer a lot of good advice.

The Twentysomething Guide to Creative Self-Employment, by Jeff Porter. Prima Publishing.

No Experience Necessary, by Jenifer Kushell. The Princeton Review/ Random House.

Generation E, by Joel and Lee Naftali. Ten Speed Press.

The Under 35 Guide to Starting and Running a Business, by Lisa Shaw. Upstart.

The Young Entrepreneur's Guide to Starting and Running a Business, by Jay Mariotti with Tony Towle and Debra DeSalvo. Times Business.

SPECIAL INTEREST

Books

The Enterprising Woman, by Mari Florence. Warner.

Most special interest books of this sort are either insipid in tone, utterly unsophisticated, or generic in spite of their title. This book is an exception, so it's worth a look.

Honey, I Want to Start My Own Business, by Azriella Jaffe. Harper Business.

Despite the unfortunate title, this book is a useful tool, serving as a sort of all-purpose shrink for couples who think they want to go into business together.

Membership Organizations

National Association of Women Business Owners. 301-608-2590. (www.nawbo.org)

This membership organization offers a number of local networking opportunities for women who own their own businesses.

Women Incorporated. 212-551-3571.

This nonprofit organization has set up a number of agreements with major banks to help women entrepreneurs gain access to loans.

HELP ON THE WAY: ACKNOWLEDGMENTS

Remember that yarn in chapter 5 about the importance of thank you notes? Well here's mine.

First of all, a big thanks to my one-time co-author and all-time coconspirator Colin Hall, who got me mixed up with this crazy business in the first place. Though he managed to weasel out of this project, he's still done more than anyone else to teach me the true meaning of the word *upstart.*

No one gets through a project like this without a plague or six of self-doubt, and I never would have been able to slog through it all without the bucking up of my close friends. Thanks to all of you, especially to Shaifali Puri and Matt Siegel, who went way above and beyond the call of duty and actually volunteered to read the thing. Also, a big tip of the cap to my editors and colleagues at *Fortune,* who have taught me everything I know about business and how to write about it. A special thanks to John Huey for shaking the place up and giving the upstarts on staff a chance to show their stuff in the magazine.

In the course of stalking Suzanne Oaks, editrix extraordinaire, I did a thorough background check before finally cornering her at a party one night in 1996. Thankfully, she didn't flee in horror (though she probably should have), and working with her has been a true pleasure. Memo to Broadway head honcho Bill Shinker: When does she get her own imprint? Thanks also to Suzanne's assistant, Ann Campbell, and to Trigg Robinson for taking a keen interest in this title early in the process.

Of course, this book wouldn't exist without the entrepreneurs whose words form its core. They invited a perfect stranger into their midst to ask hours of impertinent questions, and none of them complained a bit. All of you are truly inspirational, and I hope it shows in these pages. Unfortunately, I had to leave my favorite entrepreneur of all out of the book. That's because she's my agent, Anne Edelstein, a cheerleader, strategist, and big pill of Prozac all rolled into one. Her assistant Joanna Rakoff has been a huge help throughout.

Finally, Mom, Dad, Stephanie, David, Bramsons, Stones, and my extended California family—no matter how many more books you suffer through with me, I'll never run out of ways to thank you for your endless love and support.

INDEX